P9-DZO-193

AMERICA'S STRATEGIC FUTURE

Recent Titles in
Contributions in Military Studies

Passchendaele and the Royal Navy
Andrew A. Wiest

The Founding of Russia's Navy: Peter the Great and the Azov Fleet, 1688–1714
Edward J. Phillips

The Specht Journal: A Military Journal of the Burgoyne Campaign
Helga Doblin, translator

Collective Insecurity: U.S. Defense Policy and the New World Disorder
Stephen J. Cimbala

Communist Logistics in the Korean War
Charles R. Shrader

The Rebirth of the Habsburg Army: Friedrich Beck and the Rise of the General Staff
Scott W. Lackey

Explorations in Strategy
Colin S. Gray

The United States Army and the Motor Truck: A Case Study in Standardization
Marc K. Blackburn

Ace in the Hole: Why the United States Did Not Use Nuclear Weapons in the Cold War, 1945 to 1965
Timothy J. Botti

Counterinsurgency in Africa: The Portuguese Way of War, 1961–1974
John P. Cann

Germany's Panzer Arm
R. L. DiNardo

General William Maxwell and the New Jersey Continentals
Harry M. Ward

AMERICA'S STRATEGIC FUTURE

A Blueprint for National Survival in the New Millennium

HUBERT P. VAN TUYLL

Contributions in Military Studies, No. 169

GREENWOOD PRESS
Westport, Connecticut • London

Library of Congress Cataloging-in-Publication Data

Van Tuyll, Hubert P.
America's strategic future : a blueprint for national survival in the new millennium / Hubert P. van Tuyll.
p. cm.—(Contributions in military studies ; ISSN 0883–6884, no. 169)
Includes bibliographical references (p.) and index.
ISBN 0–313–30674–5 (alk. paper)
1. United States—Defenses. 2. National security—United States. 3. Political instability. 4. World politics—1989– I. Title. II. Series.
UA23.V293 1998
355′.033073—DC21 98–10831

British Library Cataloguing in Publication Data is available.

Library of Congress Catalog Card Number: 98–10831
ISBN: 0–313–30674–5
ISSN: 0883–6884

First published in 1998

Greenwood Press, 88 Post Road West, Westport, CT 06881
An imprint of Greenwood Publishing Group, Inc.

Printed in the United States of America

The paper used in this book complies with the Permanent Paper Standard issued by the National Information Standards Organization (Z39.48–1984).

10 9 8 7 6 5 4 3 2 1

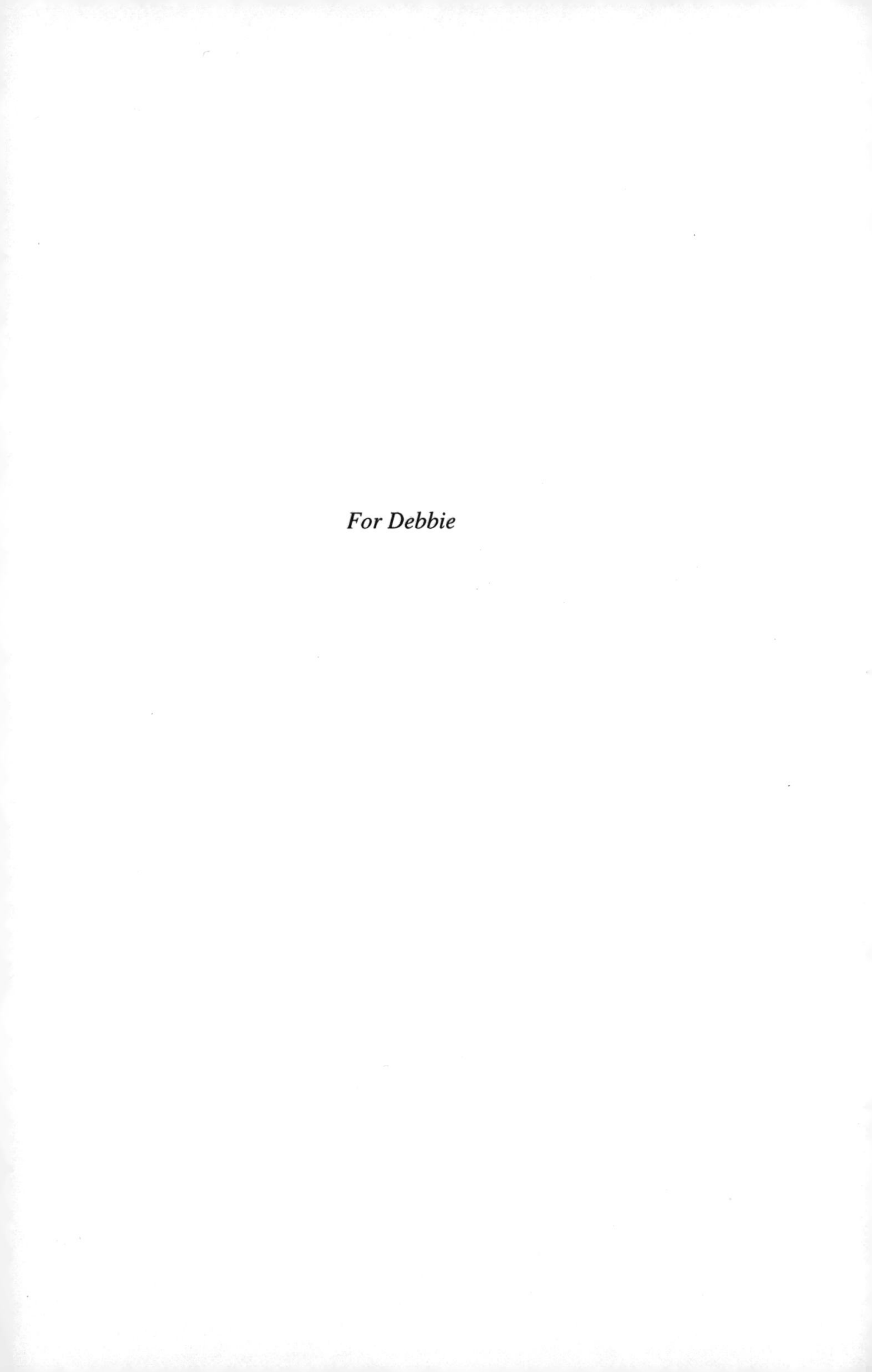

For Debbie

CONTENTS

ACKNOWLEDGMENTS

Books should be a labor of love if the reader is to experience anything positive. This book certainly was, in several ways. Strategy as a topic has fascinated me since my high school days, when I began reading military history, both good and bad, as a form of escape. For many years I had hoped to write a book about strategy, and to write it for an audience other than small communities of technical specialists. Supportive colleagues and, more important, a patient spouse finally gave me the chance to sit down and write it. But this book was also a labor of love because it is intended to help safeguard my family's adopted homeland.

Many have contributed to this book. My wife, Debra Reddin van Tuyll, and my daughter, Laura, have tolerated my physical and mental absences during the writing process; Debbie also edited the manuscript and translated much of my academese into English. My department heads, Ed Cashin and Wayne Mixon, have been invariably supportive of my pursuits, and I owe them a great debt of gratitude. Not the least of their contributions has been to give me the opportunity to teach some broad military and diplomatic history courses, which experience led me to refine many of my ideas. Finally, I need to express a special debt of gratitude to Roger A. Beaumont, whose unparalleled ability to bring a seemingly endless series of factors to bear on the massive and chaotic quantity of information that accompanies crises and wars has been an inspiration throughout my career. Neither he nor anyone else bears any responsibility for the mistakes and omissions in this book.

INTRODUCTION

The world is a dangerous place. The history of humanity has been a history of warfare, destruction, and the occasional obliteration of a nation, and, what is more, our advanced twentieth-century civilization has been more bloodthirsty than earlier, supposedly more primitive, periods. The two world wars spawned violent totalitarian movements, consumed a hundred million people, destroyed nations, and left the world on the edge of nuclear destruction for a half century. Superficially the situation today looks less dangerous. Many international organizations and treaties exist to prevent such catastrophes. Treaties and organizations, however, are weak barriers against the tensions and passions that ignite global conflicts. The period between the world wars, for example, contained an unprecedented number of peace and arms control agreements, none of which prevented the outbreak of World War II. The growth of global trade and capitalism might not prevent conflict either. Before each world war, Germany and Russia were each other's largest trading partners, but this did not prevent them from going to war; indeed, in each case, the wealthier, more capitalist state, was the aggressor.

Americans are understandably unexcited by this subject. National security is no longer a hot topic now that the Cold War is over. Geography and a legacy of immense economic and military power have made Americans feel invulnerable. During the Cold War, this feeling of invulnerability declined due to fear of nuclear annihilation and communist subversion, but these fears have dissipated, at least for the moment. The Vietnam War led to much discussion of the limits on American power to influence every global event, but not much about whether the survival of the country was a serious problem. This is unfortunate because economic and military supremacy can be nothing more than transitory phases of history, and geographical isolation cannot protect a country whose natural resources and markets lie overseas. In addition, survival means more than continued physical existence; it means that the essence of a nation, its culture, its political system, its way of living and believing are preserved. A series of crises or unsuccessful wars can cripple a nation, even if it remains physically unmolested.

This century has seen two notable examples of this admittedly obvious statement. The impact of World War I was felt far beyond the battlefield, not only in space, but also in time. The war profoundly affected the art, literature, politics, and national psyche of all the combatants, be they winners or losers. This cannot be attributed to the direct costs of the war alone. The war's battlefields took less of a toll than the 1918 influenza epidemic (although the latter's effects were spread among more nations). Instead, the long-term effects of the war can be attributed to two things. First, the conflict developed in completely unexpected directions, taking much longer than anticipated and making a mockery of war as a chivalrous contest between cleverly maneuvering adversaries. The world was treated to ghastly, gas-filled trenches occupied by soldiers dressed (by 1916) in so much protective gear as to look like beings from another planet, who were sacrificed in greater numbers and with fewer gains than ever before. Second, the war undermined traditional institutions and popular faith in them. Aristocratic, traditional Europe died a cultural death and it is small wonder that people sought solace in ideologies that offered alternative ways of organizing society. These ranged from the benign (social democratic parties like Britain's Labour) to the homicidal (Nazism and communism) with the repressive fascist parties occupying various places on the violence scale. These tendencies were not limited to countries that had suffered on the battlefield. Fascism survived longest on the Iberian peninsula, even though Portugal had taken only a marginal part in the war, and Spain none at all. The massive expansion of the Ku Klux Klan in the United States in the 1920s should also be considered.

The other example of the cultural impact of war centers on the United States. The Cold War led America to develop a "national security state" that has had an impact that virtually all analysts consider profound—but is difficult to pin down because of the recentness of the event. During the

Cold War, the United States saw itself as threatened, and the fear— some might say, paranoia—about the communist menace reached tremendous proportions. Loyalty oaths were required (and in some places still are). A huge portion of the government operated in secret. Hunts for communists threatened freedom in academia and in the arts. Americans became a majority church-going people. The words "under God" were added to the Pledge of Allegiance. America won the Cold War, but the Cold War demonstrated once again that victory over an enemy and survival (preservation) do not automatically coincide.

The twentieth century also brought a new danger: the crisis. The advent of electronic communications meant that decisions had to be made much faster, without the time to think about the implications or what alternatives might exist. Military technology has worsened this problem. The railway, airplane, and missile accelerated the pace of war and once more increased the pace at which decisions had to be made. As a result, countries can be dragged into confrontations not necessarily desired by any of the participants. This was true, for example, of the outbreak of World War I (1914) and the Cuban Missile Crisis (1962). In the former case, a disastrous war occurred, while in the second, war was avoided. But recent evidence shows that it was a very close thing, despite the fact that neither the United States nor the Soviet Union was plotting to start World War III. Unbeknown to the United States, the Soviet Union had a large number of atomic bombs in Cuba (some sources estimate over ninety). In addition, the Politburo had authorized the local Soviet commander to use his weapons if necessary. That authorization was held up on the personal initiative of the Soviet defense minister, and while the document awaited his signature, the crisis was resolved—but barely.

Wars are probably inevitable. Whether they result from the innate nature of human beings or from behavior taught by society is academic. As of mid-1997, wars[1] were in progress or in in a state of temporary truce in southeast, south, and central Asia, the Middle East, north, west, and east Africa, South America, Central America, and southeastern Europe. The odds of the United States avoiding involvement in all present and future conflicts are remote. Fortunately, these conflicts do not have to be total wars. The history of warfare has been a history of limited wars. Wars for the total conquest or destruction of the enemy are simply too

---

[1] In this context, including revolutions.

costly and risky to be undertaken on a regular basis. On the other hand, the twentieth century has seen a tendency toward total war (best exemplified by World War II) and the threat of the ultimate total war, nuclear annihilation. Even so, if this historical record still means anything, conflicts and crises can be kept at a survivable level.[2] The obvious question is how exactly to accomplish this.

The purpose of this book is to suggest strategic principles through which the United States can cope with international crises, avoid wars, and, in a worst-case scenario, survive—and win them. While this is not strictly a work of history, historical examples will be used liberally throughout to explain the bases of the various principles discussed. After reviewing why we live in an especially perilous time, I will review means of surviving a crisis, preparing for crises and wars, maintaining freedom of action, and refining the decision-making process. I will also discuss our national strategic problems and weakness.

Finally, I will propose a total of twenty-six recommendations[3] for solving our current dilemma. While nations sometimes survive crises and wars through good fortune, such as adversaries' mistakes, it would be folly to rely on luck for national survival. This is especially true in the dangerous time that we now inhabit, which makes crises and confrontations even more likely and dangerous than they were during the Cold War. It is to the nature of the dangers facing us that we now turn.

---

2. Atomic weapons may even be a benefit here because, as long as they are not used, they compel nuclear powers to limit their wars.

3. The recommendations are discussed in Chapter 7. For an overview, see appendix.

1

A DANGEROUS TIME

America is less secure today than ever. While American military power seems unchallengeable and the American economy has no equal, global affairs are now so unstable, and the future is so unclear, that the long-term security of this country is uncertain. When it comes to war, peace, and survival, real choices must be made, and they must be made now. The choices will determine whether the United States will be powerful or powerless, prosperous or poor, and independent or dependent, for the next hundred years.

The reason for this is fairly straightforward. The global balance of power is going through changes and adjustments that have few parallels. Only three times in modern history have world affairs been as unstable as they are now. First in 1789, the French Revolution overthrew a monarchy and a privileged class of people while unleashing new ideas about politics, society, and war. At first, the revolution seemed to steer France toward a constitutional monarchy like Britain's, but instead, the revolution turned radical and soon challenged the very existence of monarchy and aristocracy, the authority of the Roman Church, the patriarchal nature of society, and all established privileges. The revolution introduced political commissars, political executions, and the spread of political ideas through military force and foreign popular revolutionary sympathies. "Global interdependence" has become such a 1990s mantra that it is easy to overlook the fact that interdependence existed 200 years ago, and that the effects of the French Revolution could not be confined to France any more than the collapse of the Soviet Union will affect only Russians and their neighbors. In fact, the French Revolution triggered not only European wars, but led to two American wars, successful independence revolutions in most of Latin America, and British conquests in Africa. Once begun, the French Revolution could be neither stopped nor steered, but instead produced global instability.

Then in the 1920s, in the wake of World War I, there arose the destructive forces of fascism, communism, Nazism, and militarism. This mix of radical ideologies would inevitably have produced warfare and conflict (not necessarily World War II and the Holocaust; that would require the unique contributions of Adolf Hitler and Nazism). All four of these ideologies saw the world in terms of conflict, although the nature of the conflict was seen differently in each camp. Nazism emphasized race, communism focused on class, militarism stressed national interest, and fascism saw a struggle between order and chaos (represented by left-wing radicalism). The conclusion of each ideology was essentially the same in one sense: Conflict was the natural order and should not be avoided if it becomes necessary. This did not mean that all four camps were equally aggressive. Nazism was clearly the most warlike, while communism and some fascist movements preferred to avoid war. Nevertheless, with a conflict-oriented mentality, the long-term prospects for peace were very poor even before Hitler became master of Germany in 1933.

Finally, after World War II, global stability collapsed as the great colonial empires declined and the Cold War began. The United States and the Soviet Union were ideologically completely incompatible and became implacably hostile. The wartime alliance fed, rather than reduced, this hostility. While a crude stability reigned along the iron curtain in Europe, the instability of the post-colonial era created numerous possibilities for crises and wars that could drag both superpowers in. This era was made more frightening by the existence of atomic weapons, although these also reduced both governments' desire for open warfare (especially with each capital city as a prime target). The presence of competing ideologies made the Cold War somewhat like the interwar era, with one important difference: The ideologies of the latter period were better established, and this may have made the international scene somewhat more stable (but not much).

Our current era is every bit as unstable as the other three, and even more dangerous because of the spread of nuclear weapons and the existence of terrorism. When the Cold War ended and the Soviet Union dissolved (1991), the likelihood of crises and wars increased, rather than decreased (as many had expected). The Cold War had imposed a crude stability on world affairs, dividing nations into "free," "communist," and various degrees of "nonaligned." This made foreign affairs a more straightforward business than might otherwise have been the case. All three terms were misleading. "Free" could refer to either politics or economics, and seemed misapplied when Latin American dictatorships such as the Nicaraguan Somoza regime were included. "Communist" was used in America more as an insult aimed at left-wing governments and movements than as an accurate description, and it suffered from a rather obvious defect; even the Soviet Union was not, in reality, a communist state. The "nonaligned" countries were merely those that avoided formal links to either superpower but included many sympathetic to the Soviet Union. American officials, at least publicly, glossed over these complexities. America placed every conflict and crisis into context of the U.S.-Soviet conflict; it made world affairs look comprehensible. The results, however, could be unfortunate. The United States irritated its allies more than its enemies with this simplistic approach. Latin American revolutionaries were labeled "communistic" on slender (if any) evidence with little appreciation for the political and economic motivations of the rebels. America's wealth and power, however, tended to vitiate the worst effects of this type of error—at least until Vietnam.

The claim of stability for the Cold War might seem exaggerated. The Cold War era included two bloody wars, Vietnam and Korea, as well as a host of lesser-known wars, civil wars, and revolutions across all continents. None, however, escalated beyond the regional level. The Korean War was fought on terrain adjoining China and the Soviet Union and was the most dangerous as far as escalation risk went, but the war remained limited. The Vietnam War, which receives much more American attention today, was actually less dangerous to global peace. The war was farther from the Soviet Union, most of the fighting was fairly far even from China, and the United States was not surprised by the war, as it had been in Korea. Confrontations in 1956, 1962, 1970, and 1973 did include threats of war,[4] but none turned into all-out war.

---

4. In 1956, the Soviet Union threatened nuclear war when Israel, France, and Britain attacked Egypt. At virtually the same time, the Soviet government crushed an uprising in Hungary, which raised the fear of war in Europe. In 1962, the Soviet Union and the United States nearly went to war when

The United States and the Soviet Union avoided direct conflict because they understood each other, albeit imperfectly, and shared a common interest in keeping the confrontation within limited bounds. Neither could count on "winning" a nuclear war, which would benefit only survivors in other countries (if there were such survivors). Both did dabble with nuclear war-fighting scenarios. The Soviet Union invested heavily in civil defense and developed weapons of a size most useful against "hardened' targets" such as missile fields, leading to fears in America of a Soviet first-strike capability. In reality, the size of the bombs may have been a compensation for inaccuracy. In the United States, a small group of theorists (of whom Herman Kahn was the best-known) examined various possibilities under which a nation could fight and win a nuclear war. These views appeared to gain some currency during the Reagan administration. Unlike in conventional war, however, there were simply no data on which to base projections about nuclear war. A Pentagon aphorism of the 1960s went: "No one has looked at this problem from underneath a mushroom cloud."

The atomic bomb was not the only reason that both superpowers had adopted defensive strategies. The United States' posture almost mandated a defensive strategy, notwithstanding occasional rhetoric about liberating communist territories. After World War II, America dominated every part of the world that was worth dominating or that was strategically or militarily necessary, whether for positioning military forces, access to markets, or as sources of raw materials. In Europe, the Iron Curtain divided Europe not only into communist and free areas, but also into rich and poor parts; ours was the rich part. In Asia, the United States dominated Japan and had high hopes for influence on China until the Chinese Communist Party's victory there in 1949. In other words, the United States could not possibly have improved its position in the world after World War II through offensive warfare. American Cold War leaders generally understood this. Harry Truman, the first Cold War president (1945–1953) favored a limited military buildup and only flirted with an "offensive" strategy during the Korean War when the North

---

the United States discovered Soviet missiles in Cuba. In 1970, a Soviet-backed Syrian invasion of Jordan caused the United States to go on full nuclear alert. In 1973, Egypt and Syria attacked and nearly defeated Israel; when Israel successfully counterattacked, the Soviet Union threatened war in case Israel overran Egypt.

Korean army collapsed and the opportunity to liberate North Korea was too enticing to ignore. The disaster that followed taught Truman the danger of an offensive strategy. General Douglas MacArthur was somewhat slower to learn this lesson, which is why Truman had to cut short MacArthur's military career.

Paradoxically, the Soviet Union's strategic posture was also defensive, at least militarily. The Soviet Union's orientation was never offensive in a military sense. This is much clearer now that it was forty years ago, when the Kremlin's massive land forces appeared to threaten Europe. Of course, as a self-proclaimed revolutionary state, the Soviet Union could hardly accept the international status quo. To do so would have made a mockery of its revolutionary ideals. Recent research in the now-open Soviet archives has revealed more than ever the tension between being a revolutionary force and functioning as a traditional state. The Soviet Union had to negotiate with and occasionally trade benefits with states it was technically sworn to destroy, and it had to insist on its rights under a system of international law it condemned. These were not theoretical issues. Lives were lost in internal struggles, and bitter debates within the Kremlin keep ensued.

Even so, the Soviet Union's well-developed fear of attack and invasion made it concentrate on defense and it did not, fortunately, translate its paranoia into a preemptive attack strategy. Instead, the Soviet Union cautiously expanded its influence through propaganda and subversion while feverishly trying to close the military/technological gap—but to ensure survival, not to start World War III. Ever since the 1920s, prominent Bolsheviks had criticized those who wanted to wage war to export revolution as "adventurists" and sometimes executed them. Stalin felt that war might risk the gains the Soviet Union had made, including its advance to superpower status after World War II. The Soviets were also acutely aware of the costs of war; the Soviet Union lost about 27 million people in that war, compared with some 400,000 American fatalities. In sum, while the Soviet Union was "only" number 2 in world power after the war, this was a considerable improvement over its prewar status, albeit an improvement won at dreadful cost. The Soviet Union therefore also had little to gain from offensive warfare.

This lack of interest in attacking was partly based on two related fundamental assumptions of Marxist, and hence Soviet, thought. First, the capitalist states were expected to collapse. They might do this through war, and some Marxist thinkers saw each world war in this context. Second, the capitalist states might suffer an economic crisis that would topple the entire capitalist system. The Great Depression had not accomplished this, but as economic crises in capitalism are supposed to get progressively stronger (according to Marxists), the future looked bright. After World War II this viewpoint was strengthened by the disastrous economic condition of Western Europe, and the apparently high Soviet economic growth rate. These perceptions turned out to be grossly inaccurate. Western Europe recovered quickly, and Soviet economic performance did not match Soviet government claims. The CIA estimated in the 1970s and 1980s that Soviet GNP was only 25 percent of American output; recent estimates put the figure at 14 percent. Even so, the high growth rate of the 1950s and 1960s, coupled with problems in America, helped convince Kremlin leaders that offensive warfare had little to recommend it—a viewpoint that coincided with their own instinctive outlook.

The net result was that a kind of stability existed at the world's major "flashpoints." Both superpowers, for example, would be involved in Middle Eastern crises, but neither especially wanted those tussles to spill over into regional or global war. Korea and Vietnam provided the Soviet Union golden opportunities to make life difficult for the United States (and why should it have done otherwise?) but nothing more, despite the proximity of Korea to the Soviet border. No such certainty exists today regarding the world's known flashpoints, such as southeastern Europe, central Asia, the Middle East, or— by far the most dangerous—East Asia, where the increasing belligerency of a powerful but unstable China is generating great nervousness. No one can say for sure whether China is merely playing a game of nerves; neither can we do much more than speculate about the limit to which China might escalate. China has so rarely played an aggressive role even in regional affairs that there are no meaningful precedents. Its policies are no longer tied to those of another large communist state (as was the case during the Cold War), and its government is wobbly over the long term, making its behavior especially unpredictable.

The reason for Chinese long-term instability lies in its financial sector. As was true in the Soviet Union, a majority of state enterprises (which employ most urban workers) are money losers. The Chinese government wisely no longer subsidizes these enterprises directly, but its state banks have lent heavily to these troubled organizations. If the latter collapse, the banks will go, too. In addition, because of slow, partial privatization, Chinese managers (following the Russian example) have acquired the best parts of many enterprises themselves, leaving the less efficient parts for the state and the public to support. In a worst-case scenario, the Chinese currency could collapse. It is worth noting that the French Revolution, the rise of Nazism, and the Bolshevik Revolution were all aided significantly by the collapse of, respectively, the French, German, and Russian currencies.

The instability in all areas is increased not only because Cold War balances of power have disappeared, but because all other potential factors for conflict are present in all of these regions. Conflict requires only one government to decide that the risk of war is less of a worry than the disadvantages of the status quo. In the past, such a government would have had to secure backing from a superpower before it acted. For example, Kim Il Sung, the dictator of North Korea, had to get permission from both Mao Ze Dong and Josef Stalin before attacking South Korea. A public driven by Cold War paranoia suspected that Stalin was intimately involved in planning the conflict; academic researchers concluded that he was not. The public turned out to be right. The Soviet archives have revealed that Stalin was enthusiastic and planned the details with Kim. The idea, however, came from Kim, and whether Stalin would have approved if he had known that America would intervene is doubtful. Revolutionary movements also sought foreign assistance, and had to submit partially to the views of their sponsors. No such external restraint exists today. The major powers have been able to impose some stability in a few of the more notoriously unstable regions of the world, but no one can say for how long, or whether the amity between America and Russia will last long enough to have a significant long-term impact.

The three major periods of modern global instability noted previously should not fill us with much hope. First, all three led to war and global conflict. The French Revolution led to twenty-three years of war in Europe (1792–1815) and made warfare far more brutal and "total" than it had been in the previous century. Even the United States became involved, despite its geographical isolation. The War of 1812 flowed directly out the wars of the French Revolution. By 1812, the United States was fed up with British seizures of American sailors (drafted into the Royal Navy) and believed that Britain was so tied up fighting the French that it could not defend Canada (a major American miscalculation, as it turned out). The crises of the 1920s and 1930s, the period separating the two world wars, led to war in Asia (1937) and the outbreak of World War II in Europe (1939) and in the Pacific, when Japan bombed Pearl Harbor (1941). The Cold War resolved itself less spectacularly, as there was no direct total global war, but the Vietnam and Korean conflicts were the fourth and fifth largest wars in American history, as measured by casualties. Neither does this include the countless "police actions" and minor interventions, as well as proxy wars and fights for and against revolutions, or the many crises that nearly led to global war. In other words, all three periods of modern global instability resulted in one or more major wars, and all three involved America. There is no reason to believe the modern era of instability will be different, and the hope that America can choose to be uninvolved is simply ahistorical. In all three periods, there were always those who saw war as preferable to the status quo, simply because that status quo was unacceptable. That is still the case today. Violent conflict continues in Cambodia, Peru, Colombia, and Burundi, and will probably shortly recur in Bosnia and its environs.

A second reason for pessimism is that the dangers of instability were understood quite well by the major powers of the day, but they could do little to prevent disaster. During the French Revolution, Austria and Prussia invaded France to crush the uprising and restore order. Besides desiring to place the French king back on his throne, the invading powers hoped to contain the contagion of revolution. The result was that the French utterly defeated the invaders and then counterattacked and conquered Europe themselves. After World War I, an exceptional number of peacekeeping efforts occurred. These included the formation of the League of Nations, naval arms-limitation treaties, and military alliances and buildups aimed at deterring or stopping the aggressive tendencies of Nazism and fascism. Britain and France have been much criticized for their failure to stop Nazi aggression. The United States, however, was no more successful in deterring Japanese aggression in the Pacific. America's costliest Cold War conflict, Vietnam, was hardly a surprise; the region had been at war more than twenty years before the American entry, but the United States could not prevent its slide into the quagmire, could not foresee the problems, and could not establish (or even define) the conditions of victory.

Why not? Many commentators have placed the blame on circumstances of domestic U.S. politics, the (in)capacity of particular civilian or military leaders, or the failure of America to understand the difference between communism, old-fashioned imperialism, and ordinary local revolutions. Some of these allegations may be true, but they miss the crux of the matter: Even when the risk of war has been quite visible and predictable, contemporaries have not been able to prevent war. If a third reason is needed for pessimism, this is surely it. Peacemaking efforts, whether to prevent wars or to stop them, have not been overly successful.

True, there have been cases in which governments have prevented war, but these are obscured by the occurrence of titanic conflicts. The three earlier periods of global instability all included or produced peacemaking efforts with mixed results, at best.

The explanation for this lies in something understood long before the era of world wars and weapons of mass destruction. Since the beginning of the nineteenth century, diplomats and soldiers have learned that treaties and international peace agreements are pebbles tossed into the rivers of change. Political movements, especially fanatical ones, cannot be halted by the stroke of a pen. Revolutionary movements attack the status quo. That is their nature. No revolutionary movement particularly trusts the international "order," and every revolutionary movement attacks at least one government. Revolutionary movements are not likely to honor agreements made by the very governments they despise and denounce. Of course, this problem extends to broad social and economic trends as well. Peace by definition means and requires stability, and change undermines stability; change therefore increases the likelihood of war.

The fact that change and extreme ideas can produce instability and even violence is not modern. The Romans understood it perfectly well. This is why they sought to suppress Christianity in A.D. 250—not because it was a new religion, but because it claimed to be exclusive, and hence was seen as divisive. The religious violence in Europe between the thirteenth and seventeenth centuries provides an object lesson every bit as chilling as the Holocaust of what people are capable of. Not only were dissidents executed in large numbers, but the civilian populations during the religious wars were routinely slaughtered—particularly adult males, although women and children certainly did not fare well. More than once the Church gave its sanction to mass slaughter in the midst of religious war. In the eighteenth century, however, the violence was reined in a bit as warfare became more precise and formal, killing soldiers as always but leaving the rest of the country a little less devastated. Rulers in eighteenth century Europe waged war, but they did not wage total war. The pressure for peacemaking as such did not really exist (except among taxpayers, but as most of these had no voice yet in continental governments, their influence was negligible).

The era of the French Revolution changed all this and explains both the need for, and the failures of, peacemaking. The French Revolution toppled the old order in France, unleashed nationalism all over Europe, and precipitated twenty-three years of intermittent warfare that did not end until 1815. The task of rebuilding the wreckage fell to the first modern international peace conference, held at Vienna, Austria, in 1814–1815. The statesmen assembled there that the only hope for saving order was the maintenance of peace, and they therefore had a common goal, born not of pacifist philosophy but of the pragmatic need for survival (an issue that resurfaced in the age of atomic weapons). Their understanding of survival was sophisticated. Klemens von Metternich, the architect of the post-1815 settlement, was not a blind worshipper of monarchy or other ancient institutions. Rather, he feared that the instability brought on by war might destroy society—a conservative, but not necessarily reactionary, argument. War meant destabilization, which meant revolution. Peace, in other words, was a means to an end. Peace would exist so long as governments were insecure, and so long as none would particularly benefit from war. The insecurity lasted for about three and half decades, after which governments did indeed become more adventuristic and willing to take risks. The insecurity was compounded by the uncertainty of alliances. Alliances could and did shift quickly, and no nation wished to tie its survival to the foreign policy vicissitudes of another. The pace of communications and war still allowed for such a system, in which governments did not feel the need to have complex alliances at the beginning of a conflict, and had the luxury of time to negotiate during confrontations. More important, aggressive war was extremely risky, as success invited counter-alliances. After the revolutions of 1848, however, governments felt politically somewhat more secure (most had survived the turmoil) and were more willing to engage in threats and risky diplomacy. Metternich's system did not collapse overnight, however. No total war occurred until 1914. The Crimean war (1853–1856) cannot be compared in scale with the pre-1815 and post-1914 wars. Prince Otto von Bismarck's aggressive policies led to three wars between 1864 and 1870, but his aims were limited, and it was his successors whose greater feelings of security (military prowess with little fear of internal revolt —coupled, paradoxically, with paranoid fears of Germany's neighbors—helped them plunge Europe into two world wars.

The "no benefit" concept—also known as "balance of power"—was more complicated. It depended, then as now, completely on a country's own perceptions and could not always be influenced by outsiders. Some statesmen at Vienna discounted it completely, believing that only a spirit of moderation and justice would keep the peace. It could work so long as a group of like-minded and mutually sympathetic statesmen ran their countries' foreign policies and thought more or less alike. National interests, however, diverged, making some conflicts inevitable.

These conflicts were more dangerous than before, because the French Revolution had combined the great emotional force of nationalism with the conscription powers of the modern state. Wars could now be fought on a larger scale, with more soldiers, weapons and equipment, than ever before. War had become potentially more devastating, and the limited wars of the eighteenth century looked more and more irrelevant.

The effects of the Industrial Revolution were particularly far reaching. Nations could put more materiel on the battlefield. More significant, war could now be waged continuously, without the traditional "fight and rest" of traditional campaigns. Industrialization added two other important factors to warfare, however. One was management, an activity (I will not say "science") that was nearly as important as the actual fighting. Military and civilian bureaucracies were organized with the capability of feeding men and materiel into the Moloch of war. The other was communications. The telegraph, not the Internet, created an electronic global village that reduced the time needed for diplomacy—and hence, decision-making.

Yet most Western nations managed to avoid long, all-out wars until 1914. European conflicts tended to be short, limiting the extent of the devastation—and thereby providing a misleading set of historical examples for future generations to follow. The United States did experience a long total war (the Civil War, 1861–1865), but its generals looked resolutely backward to the wars of the French Revolution, and even beyond (Sherman and Grant were among the few exceptions, although Sherman did quote Napoleon a great deal in his memoirs).

World War I (1914–1918) shattered the established order even more decisively than had the wars of the French Revolution and, not surprisingly, spawned even more determined peacemaking efforts than the preceding era. It is an uncomfortable thought that the time between the world wars is one of the most intense peacemaking periods in the history of all humanity. International organizations were established, such as the League of Nations, the ancestor of the modern United Nations. War was outlawed in 1928.[5] Arms-limitation treaties were negotiated. When these failed, military preparations were made by all the major powers, although

---

5. This was achieved through the Kellogg-Briand pact, which was negotiated by the United States and France and signed by every country that took part in World War II.

slowed by the Great Depression. Relations were opened or kept even with unpopular governments, such as Stalin's Soviet Union and Hitler's Germany. In the latter case, this was known as the "appeasement" policy—which superficially looks like such a ghastly failure[6] that it is often forgotten that it originated from the best of motives (peace) and for the best of reasons (the appeasers felt themselves too weak for war); that if it had been aimed at a rational and non-fanatical mind it might actually have worked; and that its opposite— threats—also failed in Europe in 1939. The United States tried and failed to head off war in the Pacific through diplomacy, economic pressure, and military threats. In other words, the peace process of the 1920s and 1930s (a period so akin to our own) included every conceivable technique, and yet it failed.

The record for the Cold War is mixed. The Soviet Union and the United States did negotiate a number of peace agreements, but these worked for a rather unique set of reasons. As mentioned earlier, neither superpower was anxious for global total war. The United States had absolutely nothing to gain, as the strength of its strategic global position was without equal in history. The Soviet Union, on the other hand, never felt strong enough to risk a direct challenge to American hegemony, and would have acted contrary to its historical tendencies if it had become aggressive on a large scale. The verdict of history will be that all the major Cold War Soviet leaders were primarily concerned with securing their own empire and its immediate environs, and only secondarily with overthrowing the West. In other words, many of the peacemaking efforts of the Cold War (treaties, military alliances, and war preparations) worked because the major players wanted them to work.

Many peacemaking efforts failed, however, such as the multiple negotiations surrounding the future of Indochina. Ironically, that conflict explains the ultimate "success" of U.S.-Soviet peacekeeping. The superpowers simply found less risky and more affordable ways of fighting each other (less risky and more affordable for them, that is) than direct global war. The United States relied on alliances, occasional direct military intervention, and arming and financing dictators to protect democracy. The Soviet Union, as befitted a self-proclaimed revolutionary state, preferred to finance and arm revolutions and revolutionary governments. There is no guarantee whatsoever that these circumstances,

---

6. As will be discussed later, recent research has rehabilitated the appeasers somewhat.

which prevented all-out war during the Cold War, will recur.

We see, therefore, three broad reasons for pessimism: All three earlier periods of global instability led to some type of war; awareness of the danger does not automatically translate into avoidance of crises and wars; and peacemaking has a mixed record at best, and is but a pebble cast into the tides of political passion and economic crisis. None of this means that we should give up and do nothing. On the contrary, the crises mentioned above should spur us to prepare to survive the inevitable crises of the future. Survival is possible. All three earlier crises ended with the defeat of the forces of totalitarian aggression. The wars of the French Revolution ended in a crushing defeat for Bonapartism (named after the French emperor, Napoleon Bonaparte); World War II destroyed the Axis trio of Nazism (Germany), fascism (Italy), and militarism (Japan); and the Cold War ended with the collapse of Stalinism, which was at least as totalitarian, if not quite as aggressive, as the others, due to its hope of overthrowing the global status quo without resort to war. In a sense, the defeats of these forces can be linked to the inherent behavior of an "aggressive" (or revolutionary) force; because it seeks to expand at the expense of an established order, it generates opposition. Napoleon secured his demise by his increasingly insatiable demands for obedience from the other European countries, and finally he was defeated in and by a recalcitrant Russia. The Axis also could not restrain its desire for expansion and brought every major state in the world into the alliance against itself. Americans are most familiar with Japan's spectacular invitation of the United States into the war (Pearl Harbor, December 7, 1941), but Germany under Hitler went further, invading, attacking, or declaring war against all the other major powers, including Soviet Russia, which defeated him. In the Cold War, Soviet Russia became the victim of this trend by alienating the other European powers through its obvious desire to communize the continent (and more).

It might be tempting to stop here and conclude that the forces of peace and freedom will inevitably defeat the forces of totalitarian aggression, but this is manifestly nonsense. For one thing, in only one of the three major earlier crises was all the aggression committed by one side —World War II.[7] The wars of the French Revolution, for example, began

7. Even here, this requires a generous reading of the Soviet Union's invasion of Poland and Finland in 1939, and the occupations of Latvia, Lithuania, Estonia, Bessarabia.

when Austria and Prussia decided to invade France, in order to put the king back on his throne (in retaliation, the French beheaded the king). During the Cold War, the United States was involved in many activities beyond its borders that can hardly be labeled defensive. Overthrowing governments (Iran, Guatemala, Chile), tinkering with foreign elections (Italy), and forming global military alliances (NATO, SEATO [South East Asia Treaty Organization], CENTO [Central Treaty Organization], and the Baghdad Pact, for examples) are not activities that can be considered purely passive or defensive.

The atomic bomb has also changed the calculus of confrontation, in some ways that are peculiar. In the crises before the Cold War, such weapons did not exist (except in the last three months of World War II), which meant that the total destruction of the enemy could be pursued with confidence. This is no longer possible, and has not been possible since 1945. The kind of conventional superiority that allowed the United Nations to defeat the Axis in World War II no longer guarantees total victory. A fanatic with atomic bombs would probably use them, especially if there appeared to be no alternative. There is also, however, a more subtle effect, which will be felt in the future: Atomic weapons proliferation may facilitate aggression. An aggressor no longer has to worry as much about generating numerically overpowering opposition because, if things go wrong, the weapons of mass destruction are there as a last resort.

Small isolated countries also benefit from the atomic bomb's nullification of numbers. Israel would hardly be pursuing as rigid a policy as is now the case were it not for its 150 Jericho I and II rockets. The major powers have not, however, been enthusiastic to share nuclear technology with their smaller allies, for two reasons. First, sharing means less control, and hence less power. Second, the small power is far more likely to actually use its nuclear weapons—not necessarily as an act of aggression, but as an act of desperation to which the small state is more likely to be driven.

The key to analyzing this type of aggressive behavior is not the terror of the atomic bomb itself, but rather what that terror represents in strategic terms. The aggressor may have no intentions of using atomic bombs at the outset. Rather, the bomb creates security; the atomic bomb is insurance against thc failure of policy. The bomb should be compared with other types of strategic "insurance" against failure. For example, a small state may secure a large ally. In 1950, Kim Il Sung decided to invade South Korea, and very nearly would have been conquered himself, had it not been for the support of Moscow and Beijing. China sent 300,000 troops to save Kim at the last moment (a counter-invasion dictated mostly by Chinese interests,[8] but that made no difference to Kim). Another example would be a state or movement that knows that its destruction would be too costly for the other side. This was the situation of Iraqi dictator Saddam Hussein in 1990. Even if the U.S.-led coalition retook Kuwait, it could not overrun all of Iraq; to do so would have upset the balance of power in the Middle East. During the Vietnam War, North Vietnam balanced itself finely between the two advantages of having a large ally and being too costly to conquer. The United States could not overrun and occupy all of Indochina, and an attempt to do so would have brought it perilously close to war with China and the Soviet Union (as well as costing it some of its allies).

The Vietnam War reminded Americans that success in war and crisis depends on many factors, not all of which can be controlled. We need to know why some nations survive and win—and the most basic purpose of victory is just survival—while others are destroyed. America's survival depends on understanding why the three earlier crises ended as they did, while keeping in mind the effects wrought by the rapid changes in our modern world. Let us begin with the most obvious and simplest question. Does survival depend upon having the most military force? Those who think so like to quote Napoleon Bonaparte, perhaps the greatest military commander of modern history: "God is on the side of the big battalions." Size is not an invariable advantage, however. First, the biggest army does not always win. Napoleon himself won many battles against the odds. When Hitler swept aside the French, British, Belgian, and Dutch armies in 1940, inflicting the most one-sided defeat in modern times, his enemies had more soldiers and tanks than he did (to be fair, the fuehrer did have the edge in airplanes).

Second, the constant maintenance of a large military complex can drain a national economy, sacrificing long-term power for short-term strength. Examples of this would fill an entire book, but perhaps the best illustration of this is Spain, a superpower in the sixteenth century, but only a second-rate power by the late seventeenth. It never recovered, as the Spanish-American War (1898) demonstrated all too clearly. Soviet Russia's collapse has been blamed (perhaps too much so) on the fact that its military spending was proportionately much higher than America's,

---

8. Possibly at Stalin's request.

while Japan and the European states benefitted from their significantly lower levels of military spending.

Third, even the largest military establishment is a useless instrument if it cannot adapt to the changing ways of fighting war. This is why "bean-counting," the assessing of military strength by counting a country's soldiers and weapons, has been correctly disparaged. Colonial armies often defeated far more numerous native armies: Cortés vs. the Aztecs, Pizarro vs. the Inca, and Clive against the Indians (the American Plains Indians reversed this trend, incidentally, killing far more than they themselves lost). The colonial victories were sometimes due to superior technology. At Omdurman (1898), the British defeated the Sudanese partly because of their possession of the Maxim gun, the ancestor of the modern machine gun. This gave rise to a piece of imperialistic doggerel:

> Whatever happens, we have got
> the Maxim gun, and they do not.

In most of the colonial victories, however, the invaders possessed advantages in morale, training, and cohesion as well; firepower alone could not explain the outcome. The biggest reason the results favored the smaller colonial armies is that the losers could not or would not adapt to new styles of warfare. A style of warfare is linked to a society's makeup and sometimes the changes needed to win a war can be so wrenching as to almost make defeat preferable. In the twentieth century, the failure of powerful armies to adapt to changing circumstances are legion; France in 1940 and the United States in Vietnam are two of the most obvious. When America entered the Vietnam conflict, its military forces were without question the world's most powerful. Yet after the loss of 58,000 lives, the expenditure of $160 billion (the most conservative estimate of the war's cost), and the dropping of more bombs than were used in World War II, the result was a communist Vietnam. Arguments about whether this result stemmed from the military's "hands being tied behind its back" miss the point. Possession of force alone will not guarantee victory if a country cannot adapt to the particular circumstances of a war.

Fourth, the maintenance of large armies can be counterproductive. Having, flaunting, and using force may intimidate and frighten other countries until they respond by arming themselves or forming alliances against you. Germany threatened its neighbors before World War I and as a result faced encirclement, the very thing the Germans had hoped to avoid. Hitler did the same. His tremendous rearmament program provoked counter-preparations in France, Britain, and Russia, and his actions strengthened the Anglo-French alliance (although he did not initially face encirclement). The Soviet Union could have undermined NATO in the 1960s by withdrawing some of its enormous army from eastern Europe. Instead, it suppressed the liberalization of Czechoslovakia in 1968 (perhaps showing the real reason that Russia's army was in Eastern Europe in the first place). The frequent American use of force has bred resentment in many quarters—particularly in Latin America—which so far has not done any lasting harm to the American strategic position. But it could.

These four reasons that force alone does not spell security are obvious enough to undermine our belief in Napoleon's cleverness. Or are they? In reality, Napoleon was far more sophisticated than a modern "bean-counter." He often won at long odds. He understood well that measuring a country's strength requires more than merely counting its soldiers and weapons. Can we solve the problem by aggregating other resources as well? It is true that in all three of our major crises, the ultimate victors did have more people, resources, and wealth than the losers. In other words, the "strong" defeated the "weak." Unfortunately, there are too many exceptions to this rule for it to be of any use: The Mongol conquest of Eurasia, the Dutch revolution against Spain, the American victory in the Revolutionary War, and the communist victory in Vietnam are but a few. In reality, there is no single way to define "strength." You cannot add a country's army and wealth to arrive at a measure of strength.

This is especially so because strength means different things in different places and times. The Mongols could defeat all opponents but had too little internal strength to keep their conquests united. Holland could defeat Spain within Holland, but could not have invaded and conquered Spain. While Britain and America suffered defeats in the Revolutionary War and the Vietnam War, neither's existence or global power status were seriously threatened. The real measure of strength must take into account the fact that countries may develop strength in different ways, that they must maintain it over time, that they must make it useable, and, most important, that they must have the will and intelligence to use that strength in a sensible and advantageous way.

"Will" and "intelligence" are two concepts that cannot be quantified, as they are part of a country's and an individual's state of mind. Without these concepts, however, there is no way to understand the whole history of conflict and its avoidance. The national state of mind is every bit as important as the national military strength, and maybe more so, because the former dictates the use of the latter. The reason that will and intelligence are so important to survival and victory can be found in the nature of war itself: War is a psychological struggle waged with physical means.

This is by no means a new idea. Soldiers, diplomats, and strategists over the centuries have understood that it was their adversaries' (and allies'!) minds that they had to manipulate, encourage, or discourage, as the situation dictated. Napoleon ("The moral is to the physical as three is to one"), Hitler, Stalin, Churchill, and Genghis Khan are but a few wartime leaders who understood the mental aspect of warfare.

Consider our three crises again. In the wars of the French Revolution, France began with greater will (revolutionary fervor) and intelligence (new fighting methods and army organization) and won, only to lose when European states' resentment of French domination exceeded their fear of French arms, and used diplomacy and better methods of warfare to destroy an overextended enemy. The overextension showed that France retained its will but that its leadership had lost its intelligence. On the other hand, those who resisted Napoleon were sufficiently intelligent to study and copy his methods (Napoleon: "These animals have learned something").

In the crises leading to World War II, Hitler gained an early advantage because his will to expand certainly exceeded his adversaries' will to contain him, and—for a while—he understood his enemies better than they understood him. Ultimately he was defeated because he sought to substitute will completely for intelligence. Extreme violence (the Blitz, the Commissar Order, the Holocaust) became his only strategic idea, and he truly forced his enemies to develop a will at least as great as his own. That will was expressed in the unconditional surrender policy enunciated by the Allies in 1942 at Casablanca. In a sense it also represented an effort to reinforce will, because Britain and America feared that without such a declaration a suspicious Soviet government might negotiate itself out of the war. We know now that such a settlement was unlikely, given Hitler's foreign policy aims, but the fear was nevertheless legitimate. Negotiations between Nazi Germany and Soviet Russia continued until the end of 1943 (not the summer, as previously thought). More important, the Soviet will to victory equaled Hitler's, and nothing other than a total Nazi retreat would have been acceptable.

During the Cold War, the United States relied on deterrence. This is the principle of using the threat of force to discourage (deter) an attack. Deterrence is completely psychological. It does not depend on your strength, but rather on what the adversary thinks your strength is. It does not depend on your willingness to use your force, but whether your adversary thinks you are willing to use your force (which is why a government that projects questionable sanity and decision-making sometimes fares better in deterrence situations than one that is moderate and reasonable). Deterrence depends completely on influencing your adversary's thinking, decisions, and attitudes.

We can use "will" and "intelligence" to analyze the outcome in Vietnam, and to combine that with a reinterpretation of the "strength" issue as well. First, the Viet Cong and North Vietnamese had an advantage in will because they had been fighting in one form or another for over 20 years before the American entry into the war and were not prepared to settle for anything less than total victory. The United States' goals in Vietnam can be charitably described as confused.[9] Second, the Viet Cong and North Vietnamese had an advantage in intelligence as well. Their leaders knew the country, the culture, and the language, and had a military doctrine of revolutionary war authored by Mao but with its roots in the works of Karl Marx's collaborator, Friedrich Engels. The United States knew far too little. For example: Were the Vietnamese enemies mostly motivated by Moscow, by Beijing, or by domestic political considerations? The answer could have dictated profound changes in strategy. Resistance to Muscovite expansion was one thing, while sending half a million soldiers to fight in a domestic civil war would be quite another. Yet the question was never clearly answered.

Finally, strength. Throughout we have referred to the United States as the "stronger" power in its conflict with the communist Vietnamese. But if we look at the strengths of the two sides, a different picture emerges. First, America's aggregate military strength meant little; what was important was how much of that strength could be used in Southeast Asia. The United States had 3 million people in uniform during the war, but only about 626,000 of them were stationed in Southeast Asia at the war's peak (the United States had other commitments, after all). The United States had enormous nuclear firepower, but this was politically unusable in Vietnam. The United States had air superiority and tremendous firepower, but two factors limited its effectiveness. First, this firepower could not be used without limits in North Vietnam. Second, the lightly armed and fast-moving enemy soldiers did not make good targets

---

9. The fact that the Rand Corporation was commissioned in the 1970s to conduct a study of what America's goals in fact were speaks volumes.

for conventional bombing. The United States did have on its side a very large South Vietnamese army, but this organization was heavily infiltrated by the enemy, equipped and trained along American lines, and of uncertain morale. Once these factors are considered, the opposing strengths are actually much closer than usually imagined.

But one additional consideration in calculating the opposing strengths decisively tipped the balance toward Hanoi: casualties. Obviously the willingness to shed your own blood is a good measure of will, but it can also be used to calculate strength as well. The United States suffered 58,000 fatalities in nine years of fighting; Vietnamese loss of life (among civilians as well as soldiers) was probably closer to 2 million. The North Vietnamese and Viet Cong never considered ending the war because of the devastation of their homeland, and were willing to suffer losses that were almost twenty times those of the United States. In some situations, a relative willingness to shed blood may not matter. In this war, it did, and it made the communist forces, not the Americans, the stronger force.

What lessons do these examples give us for today—and tomorrow?

- First, to survive, we have to know what to do, and why it has to be done. We can not prosper if we just respond to each event as it pops up; we have to make plans. This is intelligence.

- Second, we have to agree among ourselves what we have to do, and why we are doing it. During much of the Cold War, we were blessed with a national consensus. We have to create a new one. This is will.

- Third, we have to prepare, to take the military, economic and political steps to ensure our survival and security. This is strength.

None of this can be achieved, however, if we do not clearly understand the nature of war and crisis, what it takes to keep the peace, and how to build a national consensus that will give us the patience and firmness to make the world safe, not only for us, but for all humanity. We cannot do any of this without looking at the only information that we really have about how people and nations behave in crisis: the past. In the pages ahead, we will examine the issues facing us by looking at how our forebears survived or perished as the case may be during the crises of their lifetimes.

2

THE MOMENT OF DANGER

The American experience with international crises is unique. Geography and the resources to project power have given the United States the ability to choose whether to participate in a developing crisis, and when and how to jump into the midst of a war. Geography also presents some subtle disadvantages for the United States, which will be discussed at the end of this chapter. Many countries, however, would envy America's distance from adversaries.

It requires only the most cursory glance at history to discern the advantages of fighting on someone else's soil—and common sense would probably suffice to make the point. Of course, fighting abroad carries with it the problems of unfamiliar terrain, enhanced logistics problems, and political-military failures occasioned by ignorance of local conditions. These problems pale beside the benefits gained from fighting at home. Besides the obvious advantage of preserving civilian life and property, the "force-projecting" power can also cut its military losses as well, partly by having some control over when to enter and when to leave the conflict. America's 51,000 World War I battle deaths were less than one ninth those of the least hard-hit major European power (Italy). In World War II the United States lost 405,000, significantly exceeding only Italy and France among the major combatants; among the global warring states, American losses must be compared with Britain's 398,000 (suffered on a smaller population), Japan's 1.5 million, Germany's 2.9

million, and the Soviet Union's 7.5 million.

This pattern continued during Cold War fighting. The frustrations felt by Americans about the Korean and Vietnam wars did not always take into account what this country and its army were spared by fighting in Asia. The U.S. military lost 34,000 men in battle, and suffered 21,000 deaths from "non-battle" causes. The South Korean army lost 70,000 men, while the combined North Korean and Chinese armies probably suffered over half a million deaths. Finally, in Vietnam, the United States lost 46,000 men in battle (58,000 total), compared with 197,000 fatalities in the much-maligned South Vietnamese army, and as many as 900,000 deaths in the North Vietnamese and Viet Cong forces. Certainly the conflict was a quagmire, but if the United States could leave only with difficulty, the Vietnamese could not leave at all. These numbers, which do not begin to consider civilian losses and physical and economic devastation, should be considered during the debates over whether American forces should be sent overseas.[10]

This ability to stay aloof until circumstances merit involvement was apparent to the country's founders, in particular, Washington, Jefferson, and Hamilton. The few wars against foreign powers in the republic's first century all confirmed this advantage. The "Quasi-War," an undeclared naval war against France in 1798–1799, was launched while that country was deeply embroiled in European conflict, enabling the United States to prevail, and gain revenge for French seizures of American commercial vessels. Similar calculations led to the War of 1812. Britain was in the midst of a bitter conflict with France, and from the American perspective, there could be no better time to seize Canada from Britain and thereby remove a major colony on our boundaries. The timing was bad, and Britain won the war. The belief in geographical security, however, was not undermined. The United States, even in 1812, was too large and too remote for Britain to occupy or defeat decisively, and, as the 1815 postwar Battle of New Orleans demonstrated, even after a series of military disasters, the United States was still not defeated.

Until a century ago, America's military involvements were largely confined to this continent. A smattering of naval expeditions did go far

---

10. Casualty figures taken from R. Ernest Dupuy and Trevor N. Dupuy, *The Harper Encyclopedia of Military History*, 4th ed. (New York: HarperCollins, 1993) and U.S. Department of Commerce, Bureau of the Census, *Historical Statistics of the United States: Colonial Times to 1970* (Washington, D.C.: G.P.O., 1975). Vietnam loss figures vary greatly.

afield, such as the operations against pirates in North Africa in 1801–1805 and 1812, Matthew Perry's expedition to compel Japan to open its ports in 1853, and some combat at sea between Union and Confederate warships. These were relatively minor forays involving small forces and few personnel. At no time did American leaders contemplate, or have to contemplate, global military strategy.

Superficially, one exception to this would be the Monroe Doctrine, that grandiose document that demanded that colonization of the Western Hemisphere should stop (or, as cynics have put it, colonization by anybody *else*). When Secretary of State J. Q. Adams issued this pronouncement in 1823, he was thinking about the strategic benefits of not having great European powers in the neighborhood, and positioning the United States to oppose recolonization, if and when possible. Most of Latin America had become independent, and the United States wanted to make clear its preference for this state of affairs. The Monroe Doctrine anticipated the possibility of military strategy, but was not true military strategy in and of itself, except in the grand strategic sense of securing one's region from major-power intrusions. The United States, with its tiny navy (twelve frigates) and small, indifferently equipped army (not over 10,000 soldiers throughout this era) could hardly have retaliated directly against a determined colonial power's attempt to establish a beachhead in the Americas. Once Britain endorsed the Monroe Doctrine, however, the naval balance of power swung decisively in favor of the American position, and hence further contemplation of foreign adventures became unnecessary. The Monroe Doctrine would produce a great deal of military activity— but most of it in the twentieth century. Global military strategy was neither possible nor needed.

Ventures beyond North America changed the picture. The Spanish-American War was America's first global conflict, although fought against a weak and impoverished opponent. Once again, the United States chose the time and place of the conflict, declaring war and sending a fleet to attack the Philippines (although the crisis that triggered the war, the destruction of the battleship *Maine,* occurred in Cuba). When the smoke cleared, the United States had acquired Cuba, Puerto Rico, Guam, and the Philippines, thereby becoming a Pacific power and establishing an imperial dominance of the Caribbean that exists to this day. At the end of the nineteenth century, the United States had not experienced a single war or serious crisis in which it had not had the initiative.

This would change in the twentieth century, but slowly. The little-known War of the Philippine Insurrection (1898–1902, causing more deaths than the vastly better-known Spanish-American War) was a costly effort to suppress an uprising in the Philippines. It so embarrassed America that it was more or less forgotten. The feeling of "controlling" a crisis returned with World War I. It broke out in July 1914, but did not see American participation until April 1917, with combat troops not taking part in the fighting until 1918. World War I was almost two-thirds over before the United States declared war on Germany (over the same issue that had partly provoked the War of 1812 and the "Quasi-War": freedom of the seas).

America's entry into World War II was a bit more complicated. Because the Spanish-American War had gained America territories in Asia (the Philippine Islands), and the United States had commercial and political interests in China, a dispute arose between America and Japan when the latter invaded China (1937). Tensions rose until war broke out with the Japanese attack on Pearl Harbor (December 7, 1941). In Europe, the United States ignored the prewar crises and remained uninvolved when World War II broke out (September 1, 1939). After the collapse of France (May–June 1940), however, the United States began to send aid to Britain in its war against Hitler, launched the Lend-Lease program, lent Britain warships, and started to escort convoys partway across the Atlantic. In other words, the United States did become involved in the crises leading to World War II. Nevertheless, the war was more than a third over before the United States really joined, and then only involuntarily.

The Cold War was different because it represented a continuous confrontation, something America had never experienced, and this time the United States was a primary player, not an outside third party looking on. In addition, the United States felt much more vulnerable, especially since the nuclear missile had made geography less of a guarantee of security. Certainly the Cold War's impact on America was greater than that of any other conflict except the Civil War. Yet the major Cold War conflicts were fought abroad, and the sense of freedom of action (see Chapter 4) and initiative was not completely lost.

The United States entered Vietnam more or less on its own initiative. The Korean War, on the other hand, was a crisis that arose so suddenly that there was no real freedom of choice, and America's commitments in the Far East were so substantial that geography was more a hindrance than help. Paradoxically, the United States did far better in Korea than in Vietnam, even though decisions that were made over a period of months in Vietnam had to be made in hours in Korea. The latter was almost a textbook example of a modern crisis. One reason for this paradoxical contrast of the two conflicts is that the role of initiative developed quite differently. In Korea, the United States recaptured the initiative on two fronts. Politically, the United States invoked support and thereby turned a regional clash (or civil war, if one accepts Bruce Cumings' view[11]) into an international effort to stop aggression. This was a very powerful argument to a generation that had experienced Axis aggression and had seen how little had been achieved stopping it, until World War II. Militarily, American forces regained the initiative within the first months of the war by landing forces at Inchon, in the rear of North Korean forces. The communist forces nearly collapsed and a panicked Stalin asked the Chinese to send their army into Korea, which they did. Vietnam represented the reverse situation, as America's control of the initiative declined throughout the war, with only a few exceptions (such as the Christmas 1972 bombing of North Vietnam). One of the more spectacular crises was the Tet offensive of 1968, during which the United States responded fairly effectively militarily but mismanaged the crisis in Washington, so that a tactical victory in crisis became a strategic defeat.

The word "crisis" is used so often today that its exact meaning has become obscure. Every problem that attracts public attention is labeled a "crisis." The word is a handy way to attract press attention, to raise funds, or to win an election. Those who study crises for a living have developed precise definitions, but these are not widely known and hence have little public impact. Given the excessive use of the word, it is little wonder that the public is slow to react to discussions of "crises" around the world, because, to judge by the overheated rhetoric of the evening news, the whole world seems to be nothing but a series of "crises."

We should sympathize with this public reaction, but we should not ignore the harm that it causes. A passive, hopeless, or resigned attitude toward the world situation only leads to a lack of serious debate about how to avoid real crises, how to survive when they arrive, and how to look back and learn from them. This attitude also threatens democracy. A popular complaint today is that decisions are made by a Washington-based elite. True enough— but decisions will continue to be made by this elite if people remain outside the debates on foreign policy and how to use past experience to avoid catastrophe (and it will be more difficult for

---

11. See for example Bruce Cumings, *The Origins of the Korean War* (Princeton, NJ: Princeton University Press, 1981).

the government to build and retain support in a crisis). No one can see the future, but there is plenty of experience in the past to consider how we may survive a war-related crisis.

What is a crisis? For our purpose, a crisis is any event that can turn a confrontation into a conflagration. Or to put it differently, a crisis is any event that can move an international relationship from the ordinary and predictable disputes about trade, boundaries, and so on toward the use of arms. Most wars have some triggering event, although this are not necessarily right before the shooting starts. While schoolchildren are taught that the assassination of an Austrian prince was the triggering event that led to World War I, long-term factors—such as the increasing militarism of Germany, instability in southeastern Europe, and the interlocking network of military alliances—were the real causes. In the case of World War II in Europe, the rise of Hitler triggered the conflict, but prewar political and economic instability made it possible for Nazism to take over Europe's most powerful state. An event does not trigger a crisis or war unless some type of confrontation already exists. Without existing tensions a "crisis" event may not trigger anything. Many assassinations have caused nothing more than expensive funerals, and countries have resented their world position without turning to extremists and fanatics for guidance.

If war then requires a combination of two things—an existing confrontation and a crisis—can we solve the problem by simply learning about the various friction points around the world, and preparing accordingly?

No.

We cannot do this for three reasons. First, no country can prepare for every conceivable crisis. It is simply too expensive. A comprehensive list of friction points around the world would include dozens, if not hundreds, of cases, as we would have to include every boundary dispute, every unstable political or economic situation, every country in which a radical party is likely to gain power, or a revolution is a serious possibility, and so on. Very few nations have sought to prepare for and resolve all existing crises, and those that have, have usually failed. For example, Hitler's Third Reich saw itself as surrounded by enemies—a crisis in itself—and sought to crush all its enemies by force, but was itself destroyed instead.

The United States came close to preparing for every conceivable friction point during the Cold War, building up a military budget without precedent and using foreign aid to supplement its strategy. The bill for many of our Cold War activities is still coming due—for example, the long-term costs of dealing with nuclear waste leakage at the Hansford and Savannah River sites will be enormous. America today is deeply uncertain whether it should continue this role of global policeman, or whether it is affordable. In reality, it is not affordable. It would, for example, require gargantuan foreign aid budgets to head off revolutions in countries such as Mexico and Egypt, and even if this approach would work and was economically feasible, it is politically impossible. Military spending is more popular than foreign aid, but no military establishment can be ready for all types of crises, and sending it abroad to head off crises is not possible. The political resistance against even sending the military to Haiti is evidence that the public's tolerance for military adventurism is currently low.

Second, not even the ablest government can anticipate everything that might have to be done during a crisis. The range of capabilities that the United States enjoyed during the Vietnam War was truly spectacular. At least two (Navy and Air Force), and possibly three, of the uniformed services had no equal in the world. All this firepower was backed by a large intelligence establishment, a well-educated foreign policy elite, a very modern-minded defense department chief, three competent and ruthless presidents, and the finances to support the war effort. It all came to naught. The obvious reason was that all this capacity was never properly adapted to the circumstances of Southeast Asia.

Finally, we are returning to an era in which the United States is more and more likely to be drawn into crises indirectly, that is, as a third party in a conflict between two others. Trying to catalog—let alone understand —the frictions between some 200 sovereign states is next to impossible. And this doesn't even include the conflicts that might occur because of popular passions and violent political movements that can materialize seemingly overnight. Civil wars and revolutions will occur in our lifetimes in Egypt, China, and Mexico: The United States will probably stay out of Egypt if it can, will definitely be drawn into Mexico, and will probably be sucked into the maelstrom that China will become when the current regime collapses. Civil wars and revolutions are even more dangerous than confrontations between nations. They spawn fanatical and radical movements that are completely unpredictable, do not see themselves bound by any law, and are internally unstable.

The seemingly sudden rise of charismatic fanatics can make nonsense of attempts to manage crises, let alone anticipate all of them. The rise of the most (in)famous charismatic fanatic of our century is a good example of this. Hitler's rise was not foreseen, even within Germany. As late as 1928 a prominent German political scientist could speak about German politics to a British audience without mentioning the Nazis at all. Hitler's aggressive tendencies and fanatical philosophy defeated every effort to head off war, and ultimately he had to be crushed in the costliest conflict in history. Few understood that compromise and appeasement could not work with Hitler, because he represented a revolutionary force that wanted to overthrow (not merely modify) the existing world order. Such a force could never be satisfied with limited gains. The attempts to appease Hitler between 1935 and 1939 were neither stupid nor craven but simply failed to comprehend what he really represented; the appeasers mistakenly tried to compare Hitler with previous generations of German leaders.

Unfortunately, the visible and catastrophic failure to halt Hitler led postwar thinkers to fit every challenger of the established order into a Hitlerian mold. During the Persian Gulf war (1990–1991), President George Bush even described Iraqi dictator Saddam Hussein as "worse than Hitler." That statement was good politics but bad crisis analysis, as it once again encouraged people to lump all adversaries into a single simplistic category.

Bush's comment could be dismissed as harmless political hyperbole. After all, he had to build public support for sending half a million troops to rescue hapless (and oil-rich) Kuwait, and he had to say *something* that would elevate the war to the level of a moral crusade. Bush understood all too well that the nation needed a clear justification for going to war. Having lived through World War II and Vietnam, he had an exceptionally clear vision of the difference in public support between a war presented as a moral crusade and a war in which there was no effort to gain support. Saddam Hussein also provided a remarkably easy target for moral outrage. On the other hand, Bush's comment had something in common with the above-mentioned tendency of the evening news to describe every problem as a crisis. In this case, every enemy leader becomes an insane, homicidal, megalomaniac dictator (in Bush's defense, Saddam Hussein probably meets these criteria). Every conflict becomes a struggle between good (us) and evil (them).

This good/evil dichotomy is a good and necessary attitude on the battlefield. Moderation is impractical in wartime, as warfare feeds on emotion. Hatred of the enemy works well, but if the enemy is not a country or group with which you have regular intercourse, another emotional basis for the war must be found. This is why America especially needs a moral rallying cry in wartime. We have historically had so little ongoing contact with other countries that there are insufficiently well-developed hatreds to justify going out and killing their inhabitants. Japan solved this problem for us with the attack on Pearl Harbor, but the war against the Axis as a whole required something more: a moral crusade.

While a search for a moral theme for war is hardly unique, it resonates uniquely with Americans. The ideal of America as different and morally superior can be traced to the Puritan concept of the "city on a hill." This was not, of course, military strategy, but merely suggested that Massachusetts Bay should be an example to the rest of the world. The American nation adopted this powerful image to such an extent that even today incoming college students believe that this country was founded for religious freedom, curiously omitting the earliest (economic) colony of Jamestown. The nineteenth-century idea of "Manifest Destiny," that a higher power had predestined North America as a territory for the United States, fit quite well with the "city on a hill." Predestination is a Calvinist doctrine, and the Puritans were (or thought they were) Calvinists. Hence the United States made major wars better if a moral crusade existed than if "national interest" was at stake. Morality was also a justification for sending soldiers across the ocean, as the average American did not historically have a country that could be considered a "traditional enemy." The obvious and visible moral issues of the Cold War fit very well with this quasi-religious American outlook. There was, however, a problem. The very emotional intensity that sustains a nation at war, however, precludes the rational and objective thinking necessary to navigate through a crisis.

Worse, it obscured the kinds of pressures that lead to crises in the first place. Insane, megalomaniac, homicidal dictators may cause wars by themselves, but usually there is a background at least as important as the pressure of the homicidal dictator. In the case of the Gulf War, Iraq's disagreement about its boundary with Kuwait—as well as the larger question of whether Kuwait should be a province of Iraq—preceded Hussein by almost two decades, and Iraq had threatened Kuwait long before Saddam made his beneficent presence felt (during the earlier crisis, it was the British who went to Kuwait's defense). Hitler gained power in 1933 for two reasons: German dissatisfaction with the country's treament after World War I, and the Great Depression. Another insane, megalomaniac (but not homicidal) dictator, Francisco Solano Lopez of Paraguay, led his country into war against Brazil, Argentina, and

Uruguay (1864–1870) and profited from his country's relative isolation to command and justify his aggression. The fixation on finding "Hitlers" obscures the reasons that they exist in the first place. And knowing that one is faced with a dictator is not by itself very useful. Some dictators are perfectly content to govern their countries and kill their people without bothering their neighbors, while maintaining friendly relations with the United States. A good example of this is the Somoza family of dictators in Nicaragua, with whom the United States had a close (if not warm) relationship, but there were many others. The bottom line is that fixating on only the tendencies or personality of the national leader is not enough. In fact, World War I, perhaps the greatest disaster of this century, cannot be blamed on any single leader. Every putative villain turns out to have been responding to outside pressure or internal fears, and none had the megalomania of a Hitler, a Solano Lopez, or even a Saddam Hussein. How, then, can we anticipate and survive the "moment of danger" without being swept into a conflagration?

The advocates of the "peace with justice" school of thought have little difficulty with this question. Their argument—oversimplified here— is that conflict results from injustice, which they usually define in terms of poverty, hunger, and oppression. Remove these particular pressures, the argument goes, and the risks of crisis and war decline. Certainly there is a serious point here. Nations and revolutionary movements are most likely to proceed to war in a crisis if they believe that they have less to lose from conflict than from avoiding it. Modern history is rich with examples of wars caused by such an attitude, and there are even a few examples of wars avoided when this attitude was not present. In World War I, governments generally saw war as preferable to inaction, fearing that appeasement would produce oppression by unjust conquerors. In the Cuban Missile Crisis (1962), on the other hand, neither superpower was keen to upset the global order through war, and peace (barely) prevailed. An advocate of "peace with justice" might argue that fewer "injustices" would mean fewer pressures for war.

Unfortunately, much of the evidence is ambiguous. First, virtually every combatant in history has fought believing that its cause was just. It would be hard to recruit otherwise! In the American Civil War, the costliest conflict ever waged by Americans, we have a good example of a conflict in which both sides were convinced of the essential justice of their cause. Second, it is not necessarily the oppressed, the poor, or the hungry who cause conflict. Their problems could well make a society unstable, but few international conflicts can be directly attributed to them.

Poorer nations may attack richer ones, but the strong are even more likely to attack the weak. Revolutions are the ultimate destabilizers. All three of modern history's major eras of instability involved revolutions. They were not, however, made by the poorest and the most oppressed—at least not acting alone. The French Revolution began as a struggle between the monarchy and privileged nobility on the one hand and the representatives of the "commoners" on the other. But these representatives were not the downtrodden poor; more typically they were lawyers and other educated types. Nazism triumphed when the German middle classes turned to Hitler. In fact, Nazism had a respectable upper-class following. The colonial independence movements that played such a role in the post-World War II era were almost invariably led by cadres of well-educated, middle- and upper-class revolutionaries, such as Kwame Nkrumah, Mohandas K. Gandhi, and Ho Chi Minh.

Of course, all three of these revolutionary eras depended on support from the downtrodden. The French Revolution's momentum increased because of peasant violence and the demands of the Paris "mob." Nazism rose amidst the misery of Depression-era Germany. Mass support from below was necessary for independence movements to succeed. But if poor people made revolutions, the world would be in a perpetual state of revolution.

Third, who defines justice and injustice? Who decides what is just and unjust? In an international system of sovereign states, each country can decide that more or less on its own. This state of affairs has prevailed since the Peace of Westphalia in 1648, which recognized the modern international system of sovereign states, not subject to a higher earthly power. Justice would be defined for each state's citizens by that state, and each state would also define whether it was being treated justly. Justice and sovereignty were never comfortable bedmates. In essence, each state had the legal power to determine justice within its own borders, but retained the right to criticize allegedly unjust behavior elsewhere. The United States is particularly overbearing in this regard.

Revolutionary and popular movements pay even less attention to foreign viewpoints. This may not be true, admittedly, of a movement's leaders. If they receive aid and encouragement from a foreign power, that power's opinions matter. Mao Ze Dong, leader of the Chinese Communist Party, had a warm relationship with Soviet leaders and frequently modified his party's positions in response to Soviet critiques. On the other hand, the impact of these relationships may not be significant in the greater scheme of things. The United States had little success in using its relationship with Soviet Russia to gain some sort of leverage over movements supported by the Soviets. International law regarding justice has even less meaning. Revolutionaries have by definition cast off the chains of legalism and are in the process of redefining exactly those fundamental principles of law that would, ideally, form the basis for a concept of justice.

The most famous case of the problem of defining injustice can be found in Germany between the two world wars. Germans resented the terms of the Versailles Treaty (1919) that ended World War I. This resentment was fanned by the Nazi Party and used as justification for rearmament, expansion, and, finally, war. Yet what injustice had Germany actually suffered as a result of the Versailles Treaty? First, the treaty officially blamed Germany for the war—obnoxious to Germans, perhaps, but hardly a long-term crippling blow. Second, the treaty imposed an indemnity, but the Germans never paid it. Third, Germany's military establishment was sharply limited in size, but as no one attempted to conquer Germany between the wars, this hardly mattered. Fourth, the treaty stripped Germany of two pieces of territory—Alsace-Lorraine in the west, and part of the province of Posen in the east. The loss of the eastern territory angered many Germans. Yet, considering the magnitude of World War I and the immensity of the losses of the victorious powers, from a purely rational perspective Germans should have been beside themselves with gratitude over the treaty terms, which were far more generous than what the Germans intended to do to their adversaries if they won. Instead of being grateful, they turned to Hitler.

Of course, to be fair to "peace with justice" advocates, they could argue that the absence of a strong international forum for dispute resolution is what allows sovereign states to act unilaterally in deciding what is just. This is true, but only up to a point. The great conflicts of our century have been caused or stimulated by sweeping ideological movements and emotional forces that could not be restrained by international law. Diplomacy and treaties before World War I were as naught before nationalism and fear of being conquered. The numerous peace-keeping and arms control agreements between the world wars proved impotent in the face of fascism, Nazism, and militarism. During the Cold War international law was often a tool and a weapon. Communists view law as a tool of class repression, not as an objective means for dispute resolution. The democratic states, especially the Anglo-American group, had a more elevated concept of law, but even the United States was (and is) more than willing to bend and break the rules. The concept of the rule of law will have to take root firmly around the globe before it can put a stop to violent conflict between nations. Popular movements will always be even more difficult to bind in this way.

The fourth and most important reason that the "peace with justice" view does not help us much is that it does little to help us anticipate or survive a particular crisis. Most conflicts do have causes that fit in the "peace with justice" framework. Those causes, however, are omnipresent, even in the countless situations where conflict did not occur. To postulate that revolution occurs where people are dissatisfied does not explain which group of dissatisfied people will revolt. Why not? The oppressed may not have felt oppressed (and, by the standards of their time, may not have been oppressed). They may have been apathetic or hopeless. They may never have organized, so that their opposition never went beyond random acts of violence. The oppression may have been too effective for a revolution to take place. The major totalitarian states of our century faced no effective internal opposition; only moderate or incompetent dictatorships are overthrown. Finally, in the midst of crisis, it will not be the oppressed but their leaders and representatives who decide whether to escalate, and they may have their own agendas.

Yet despite all these problems, the "peace with justice" concept still has some value for understanding crises and wars, and their avoidance. When the wars of the French Revolution ended, and European statesmen struggled to stabilize the shattered continent, French Foreign Minister Talleyrand said that peace would prevail only if "a spirit of moderation and justice" flourished. This is a rather remarkable statement coming from a diplomat usually (and inaccurately) pictured as a complete cynic. Talleyrand's opinion found an echo in, of all places, the Soviet Union. Soviet military strategists believed that war could be avoided only if the "forces of peace" were strong. The existence of military force alone, they believed, would neither prevent war nor deter aggression. Talleyrand and Soviet strategists had experienced crises that could not be resolved without war, that could not be deterred, and that culminated in extraordinarily bitter conflicts. Small wonder that they had little faith in deterrence. Another good example of this is the American Civil War. It was preceded by more than forty years of debate and regional conflict over slavery, which made the war foreseeable but not preventable. Between 1865 and 1945, however, no international crisis truly threatened the United States' existence. Even the world wars were other countries' conflicts in which the United States was a late entrant. This relative immunity may explain why so much of American strategic thought ignored the possibility of a serious defeat, that is, one in which the adversary could have a direct negative impact on the United States.

This strategic myopia did not disappear during the Cold War (except in the context of nuclear war), despite its radical difference from previous American conflicts. The Cold War was a lengthy confrontation punctuated by several crises that the United States survived by a combination of geographical remoteness, superior resources, strong alliances, and good fortune. These advantages are neither eternal nor inevitable. Alliances born in the Cold War will become increasingly uncertain, and, in some cases, undesirable. Superior resources mattered when there was a single, clear, identifiable adversary, and even this advantage turned out to be dubious when an army trained to fight Russians in Germany was dropped into the Mekong Delta.

Geographical remoteness appears unchanging but is actually relative. Pearl Harbor, the missile, and terrorism made it seem less certain. More serious, however, is that geographical remoteness is a double-edged sword. First, geographical remoteness causes the nation to experience a false sense of isolation, ignoring ways in which the United States can be directly affected by affairs abroad, such as crises that might interrupt the flow of natural resources. Second, it strengthens isolationism (discussed in Chapters 4 and 6). Third, geography is no defense against a global economic crisis, as the Great Depression proved. Finally, geographical remoteness merely means that a crisis reaches the United States somewhat later than would otherwise be the case. This last point is by far the most important.

The slow(er) approach of crises creates an attitude in the United States that preparation can be put off until the crisis is clear, and that we can get involved in the crisis if and when it suits us. At least the latter view has some historical basis. As seen at the beginning of this chapter, the United States has had a fair amount of freedom to enter or avoid international crises and wars. Unfortunately, this relative success has obscured two important points. First, entering a war at a time of one's choosing does not guarantee success. Contingency preparations must be made for failure as well. Three famous wars illustrate the point. During the Peloponnesian Wars, when the ancient cities of Athens and Sparta warred, the Athenian leader Pericles began a war using a strategy that was unquestionably brilliant, but all his calculations perished (as did he) due to an epidemic that swept the city. During the summer crisis of 1914, Germany decided that 1914 was as good a time for war as there might ever be, and swept the continent (and itself) to disaster, because its foolproof war plan turned out to be not foolproof. In the War of 1812, America's calculations and strategic assumptions were sound, yet it was Washington that burned, not London. War is inherently so unpredictable that even retaining the initiative (freedom of action) is no absolute guarantee of success.

The other reason that the "wait and see" approach is dubious is that it does not reflect American military history very well. Before most of the wars mentioned in this chapter, the United States was better prepared relative to its adversaries than is generally believed. In the "Quasi-War," the United States had a very small fleet, but it was more than adequate for the job, seizing a hundred French ships and forcing France to the negotiating table. In the War of 1812, the U.S. land forces were small but numerically superior to the British-Canadian forces they had to face. In the Spanish-American War, the American forces were clearly superior at sea and a match for the Spaniards on land. In World War I, the U.S. Army was in very bad shape, but the navy was quite large and, at least on paper, ready for war. Pearl Harbor found a United States that (to Japan's misfortune) had been preparing for war for two years. Korea required considerable improvisation because of post-World War II demobilization, but the American military was hardly small in 1950. Finally, the military establishment peaked in size and firepower during Vietnam.

Preparing for a single crisis, or a select few crises, let alone in the midst of a crisis, will not work. By definition, crises contain unpredictable elements. This is even more true of wars. Nations have survived crises and wars because of one or more of the following:

- Inherent advantages that they exploited.
- Mistakes made by adversaries.
- Broad and flexible preparations that allowed for adaptation to changing circumstances.

We now turn to the question of how we ought to prepare.

3

GETTING READY

Of the three conditions necessary for surviving a crisis or war, only one can be controlled. Inherent advantages, the first condition, are strengths that the country can expect to have for the foreseeable future because they are not dependent on particular policies or events. Examples include a stronger government, greater population, larger economy, natural defenses, geographical isolation, or a popular sense of cohesion and patriotism. Long-term policy can bring about or destroy these advantages.

Long-term policy, however, is a contradiction in terms, because most decisions in crises and wars result from ad hoc necessities, not carefully thought-out plans. Plans rarely fit the exact circumstances of a crisis and are therefore supplanted by short-term decisions. The increasing pace of war and communications has accelerated this tendency. In the Berlin Blockade (1948–1949), the Korean War (1950–1953), and the Cuban Missile Crisis (1962), there was a general American policy—to stop the spread of communism—but the actual operative decisions (airlift, intervention, and blockade, respectively) had to be made in an extremely short period with little policy guidance.

Neither is there much pressure for long-term policy when it counts. The rational need for good long-term policy is often blocked by powerful competing forces that, in and out of government, strive to gain short term ends. Two examples of this are military procurement (drawn to powerful congressional districts) and the federal budget (unbalanced since 1969 because of the hunger for government services without a compensating appetite to pay for them). More to the point, there is no permanent political center that can maintain long-term policy. American political parties have degenerated into election administration machines (partly because of the pernicious effect of primaries) without much real long-term policy, and such a policy could not be enforced on candidates.

Fortunately these democratic problems are more than made up for by the stultifying effect of autocracy. Totalitarian and autocratic states lack the creativity that flows out of the chaos of a democratic culture—and hence, while they may enforce long-term policy better, they cannot change outmoded policies as quickly. Additionally, long-term policy does exist in all systems, but not always at the top, where it is usually sought: It can be found in the middle and lower echelons of an organization. In war or peace, an organization's staff and middle managers collectively are far more important than the overstudied top figures. A sufficiently aged organization has a corporate culture that resists the grand designs of presidents, generals, and so on, and it is often that culture which makes real long-term policy. The Soviet leadership could politically cow subordinates if necessary, but could not order them to reform their ways—as Khrushchev and Gorbachev found out the hard way. Academic readers might ponder the relationship between university-system chancellors and academic faculties in this context: A flow of bright and impractical ideas meets a wall of experienced professorial conservatism, which constitutes the real long-term policy of the system.

Solving these conundrums is not easy. Giving central authorities dictatorial powers (which has happened to some extent in the United States in various walks of life) is undemocratic and puts the system at risk from arbitrary decision-makers. (Major reforms can accidentally dissolve the system's glue, as Robert McNamara and Gorbachev discovered.) Using law and constitution to protect long-term policy would be better, but would increase rigidity. A system of democratic delegation might be the best way (and to some extent already exists), but understandable public mistrust of Washington would probably make it impractical to implement.

Inherent advantages cannot be changed in the short run, however. Nations change, of course, and inherent advantages may come and go. Little can be done about them in a few years, and an advantage in one situation can be disastrous in another, making it difficult to decide which "advantage" to promote. For example, patriotism and nationalism can help a country survive a crisis or a war, but can also make it too aggressive and uncompromising toward its neighbors. Without patriotism, France would not have survived World War I. Without patriotism, Germany would never have served Hitler's war efforts as loyally as it did.

Mistakes made by the adversary, the second condition, are even less predictable than best inherent advantage. Clearly many victors in war have benefited from enemy mistakes; the conflicts decided by the blunders of the losing side are too numerous to list. The victors, however, usually also committed their share of mistakes, as is inevitable given the chaos and confusion that are the defining characteristics of all wars and many crises. We have to content ourselves with a few broad generalizations.

First, mistakes will be made by all the participants in any crisis or war. America's failures in Vietnam have been well documented, for example, but the North Vietnamese and Viet Cong forces made their share as well, of which the Tet Offensive (1968) was the most frightful. Second, the adversary's mistakes are only useful if we are ready to exploit them. The United States was clearly not ready to take advantage of Vo Nguyen Giap's premature offensive in 1968 and hence turned the communist general's tactical defeat into a strategic victory. Third, an adversary's mistakes are not necessarily a good thing. In a nuclear world, this point may seem too obvious to mention. It was also true, however, before the bomb. In 1941, for example, Hitler made a "mistake" in invading the Soviet Union, but the latter country can hardly be considered a "beneficiary" of the error (27 million lives lost, and incalculable economic costs).

Fourth, the only way to minimize crisis and wartime mistakes is to prepare, in both the physical sense (strength and resources) and in the mental sense (thought and planning). The combination is essential. The United States was militarily prepared for war when Vietnam occurred, but its thinking was focused on waging war against the Soviet Union. Neither American "sense" was oriented toward Third World counterrevolutionary conflict, although the problem was not entirely unforeseen. On the eve of World War II, all major powers had begun preparing for war, yet the mental side of the equation was uneven. France mistakenly planned for defensive warfare, Germany allowed ideology to determine its evaluation of Soviet Russia, and Japan never developed a coordinated military strategy at all. This brings us squarely to the third condition for survival, the only one we can really control: Preparation.

Common sense suggests that nations which have prepared for crises and wars are more likely to control their destinies, and therefore survive, than those that have not. Even a brief glance at military history reveals that this generalization requires many qualifications. Certainly, nations that do not collectively think ahead are in great danger. Preparation and planning require time, and that is exactly what does not exist in a modern crisis. Ever since the invention of the telegraph, the internal combustion engine, and the airplane, decisions have had to be made, and actions have had to be taken, in very short time. World War II demonstrates well the need for preparation, unless an sufficient inherent advantage exists to compensate for lack of preparation. For example, when Hitler invaded the Soviet Union (June 22, 1941), he caught the Red Army almost completely by surprise; in that sense, the Soviets were unprepared. They survived and won for two reasons. First, the Soviet Union had an obvious inherent advantage in its size. Its army could trade space for time as it fell back toward Moscow while trying desperately to reorganize itself. Second, the Soviet Union's military preparations in the 1920s and 1930s had been extensive and impressive, including many innovations in tank and airborne warfare, the movement of much industry eastward, rapid force expansion, and the creation of a military organization that proved up to the task of rebuilding the army in the midst of battle—although it was a close thing. Neither Soviet blood nor Soviet space alone would have prevailed.

The American entry into World War II bears some startling similarities to the Soviet entry, although the wartime experiences were entirely different. Like the Soviet Union, America entered the war because of a surprise attack (Pearl Harbor), and, except for the Philippine Islands, enjoyed great geographical space (the Pacific Ocean). Japan could not strike the American heartland, just as Germany could not destroy Soviet Russia's industrial cities in the Ural Mountains. There the parallel ends, however. The United States did a better job of foreseeing the crisis than did Soviet dictator Josef Stalin, who was renowned for his alleged paranoia. Between July 1939 (a month and a half before World War II) and December 1941 (Pearl Harbor), the U.S. government centralized military decision-making, reintroduced the draft, placed gargantuan orders for military airplanes, and among numerous other steps, moved the Pacific Fleet to Pearl Harbor. (A minor ironic parallel: Both America and Soviet Russia moved forces close to the potential adversary shortly before war.) The move to Pearl backfired—it triggered the Japanese attack—but overall, the many American preparations go a long way to explain why the United States emerged from the war in 1945 as the most powerful country in the world, and at relatively low cost.

The emergence of America and Soviet Russia as superpowers in 1945 can be attributed partly to the preparations they made before 1941. Without those preparations, flawed as they inevitably were, the war's outcome might have been quite different. Preparedness today, however, is much more important that it was even in 1941. Most important for Americans, the inherent advantage of geography has disappeared. This is not because of technology. True, the introduction of the missile and long-range bomber technically eliminated a large part of America's geographical invulnerability, but this was not as significant as it seemed at the time.

No foreign power has attempted a serious attack against the American mainland since the War of 1812. Conventional conquest and occupation of the United States are no easier today than they were a century ago. An attacking force could cross the ocean toward America much faster today, but it would have to cope with heavy American air attacks. At the same time, the attacker would be less able to protect its attacking force the closer it got to America, because its force would be farther from its own air bases—and no foreign country has a substantial aircraft carrier force to do the job. Of course the entire country could be destroyed through aerial attack, but the attacker itself would be destroyed as well. No attack with current technology could destroy all of America's missiles and bombers, let alone the nuclear submarines.

The real reason that geography doesn't matter much any more is economic. America's enormous overseas interests have turned the United States into the modern equivalent of the British Empire. After World War II, Henry Luce, the publisher of *Time* magazine, foresaw that the United States would replace Britain in its global imperial role and went so far as to predict an "American Century" in world history. America's worldwide network of interests involved the country in numerous far-flung crises, which often had little to do with a great-power confrontation. Even the wars in Korea and Vietnam owed more to local factors than to the Cold War (the Cuban Missile Crisis of 1962, however, is a good counter-example, a crisis that could not have occurred but for the Cold War).

Luce looked backward and saw the British Empire's stabilizing influence and its immense global cultural impact. He did not spotlight the empire's long-term weakness, such as the inevitable desire of the subject peoples to cease being subjects, reflected today in American unpopularity in many global quarters. The British Empire did, however, manage to retain a major overseas presence for several centuries, despite its small army, the loss of part of North America through revolution, and the huge numerical disparity between conqueror and conquered elsewhere. This is especially relevant to the United States because Britain faced so many adversaries—and did so successfully—while trying to protect a truly global empire.

British success resulted from a pragmatic approach to empire that generally avoided ideology and jingoism (super-patriotism). Britain's empire was originally commercial, and its more intelligent leaders did not lose sight of this fact. Britain relied extensively on diplomacy, including reaching agreements with local rulers in India and Africa, without which a costly military occupation would have been necessary. In other words, Britain survived as an empire for three centuries because it did not conquer for the sake of conquest, and did not fight for the sake of fighting. At the same time, there was no particular political problem with sending the nation's servants to imperial trouble spots. An intelligent balance between expansionism and weighing its costs kept Britain as a dominating and (in Luce's view) stabilizing force—until it was effectively destroyed by German aggression.

This balance is necessary because all great empires in history have suffered from a basic contradiction: A greater empire means greater power, but also greater vulnerability. This pattern is universal and, for once, shows no exceptions. This is not surprising. A great empire, by definition, has more adversaries to oppose, more interests to protect, and more peoples to govern. The last aspect is the most important. Stable empires can protect their borders, but even powerful states may not survive internal discontent because it weakens the empire's ability to deal with its foreign problems. History is replete with examples. The Assyrian, Austrian, and Russo-Soviet empires could not withstand the pressures for independence from within while fighting external forces. The first two were destroyed by war, while the third was worn down by nearly fifty years of confrontation.

Assyria was defeated by the Chaldeans (Babylonians) in combination with revolts by its subject nations. The latter were numerous and constituted at once Assyria's strength and weakness. They were taxed to keep Assyria rich, but the costs of oppression and occupation drained Assyria's wealth and core population; clearly the costs of empire exceeded the benefits. The Austrian and Russo-Soviet cases are less clear. The Austrian empire collapsed at the end of World War I, when its fractious minorities tore themselves out of the imperial wreckage to form their own countries, which were later absorbed into the empires of Hitler and Stalin. The Austrian empire was overextended, but in a different way from Assyria. Its subject peoples had ethnic relatives in neighboring states. (This is highly relevant considering the extremist Aztlan movement in some fringe circles in the American Southwest.) Fear of its neighbors' ambitions caused Austria to pursue a war of aggression against one of its neighbors—Serbia—in 1914. The result was World War I, in which the strain of fighting Serbia and Russia proved to be too great for the weakened imperial fabric. Austria's adversaries were themselves destroyed, but at too great a cost. Austria fought to win—and did, in a technical sense, win—but collapsed in the aftermath of "victory."

The Russo-Soviet case is the most complicated because this empire's boundaries—like America's—were elastic. The Soviet Union effectively occupied eastern Europe and had major costly interests and involvements around the globe, although not on the American scale. The Soviet empire was partly ideological, and this fact involved the Soviet Union in many global activities that were not necessarily in its interests— although, to the extent that they weakened the United States, there was some benefit. The Russo-Soviet empire did not collapse, however, due to war. It won its biggest conflict. The expenses of the Cold War, however, were gargantuan, and may have crippled economic development. Unlike the Assyrian and Austrian empires, however, the Russo-Soviet state disintegrated when its ideology crumbled. Without a strong trans-national communist movement, the Soviet state proved doomed. The Soviet Union did not collapse from overextension in the usual sense of the word; neither did ethnic tensions provide the basic cause of destruction (which it did in the other two). Rather, the will to keep the empire together depended on strong communism in the ethnic republics, and strong communism in the Russian center of the country. When these conditions disappeared, there was no longer anything to keep the empire together. Whether something else will arise that can restore this state remains to be seen.

The Roman Empire suffered fewer ethnic tensions, perhaps because it lacked a clear ethnic character, but the huge cost of protecting its long boundaries coupled with fatal divisiveness in its government made it incapable of stopping the advancing Germans and Slavs. Rome's population changed due to Slavic and Germanic immigration, and this dimmed the chances for imperial survival. The new immigrants remained largely unassimilated. Emperors' reigns were too brief to make much difference. The powerful Roman Church was ambivalent about the empire. When the last Western Roman emperor was deposed in 476, it made little difference to anyone (except the emperor). Rome simply faced more numerous adversaries than it could possibly have contained, a problem complicated by the increasing obsolescence and inadaptability of its institutions.

Assyria, Austria, Russia, and Rome were "contiguous" empires, in that their colonies lay next to the homeland. The overseas colonial empires were even more vulnerable. The two largest, the British and French empires, dissolved in about a decade and a half after World War II. It made little difference whether the colonial power yielded or fought; the outcome was the same. Why was this so? First, distant colonial outposts were difficult and costly to protect adequately, especially from a competing major power. Colonial outposts changed hands throughout the history of empire. In our century, Britain seized Germany's colonies in World War I, Japan seized some of Britain's colonies in World War II, and the Soviet Union sought to capitalize on nationalism in colonies during the early Cold War. Second, the colonial inhabitants will sooner or later come to resent the mother country and will revolt. Fighting such a revolution is wildly expensive and will not change the long-term outcome. Finally, the empire is inherently dependent on the markets and natural resources provided by its territories and must protect them all—despite the expense.

Strictly speaking, the United States is not a colonial empire,[12] but it is

---

12. It depends, of course, on the definition. American Indians, for example, might quarrel on this point. Virtually every state, however, contains some peoples and territories that were, at some point, conquered. A state with a collection of a great many such peoples intuitively can be considered a colonial empire. In addition, most of the states considered colonial empires in the twentieth century have been those with overseas territories, something which the United States no longer holds. The seizure of Hawaii was an overseas colonial annexation, but that chapter in American and Hawaiian history ended with Hawaii's statehood. The Philippines were an overseas American colony, but gained independence in 1946. The remaining overseas territories include Pacific islands, many of which have become independent, and Puerto Rico. Puerto Rico could be defined as an overseas colony, but there are two problems. First, Puerto Ricans regularly vote on whether to remain part of the United States (giving Puerto Ricans a right not held by the inhabitants of any state). Second, Puerto Rico imports mainland U.S. wealth while exporting people there, exactly the reverse of the traditional colonizer/colony relationship.

an overseas empire, with all the vulnerabilities that come with that status. Defense of America's global interests involves fantastic costs. Resentment of American influence and military power exacerbates crises. Dependence on imported oil (and other natural resources) requires military readiness to secure the oil flow in such dangerous places as the Persian Gulf. There is hardly a place on the globe where the United States does not have "interests" of some type. Therefore, the United States must be exceptionally well prepared to cope with crises— that is, to be ready. But what does this mean?

As discussed before, quantity and quality of military forces alone are not enough. A big army is a comforting (if costly) possession, but if it is used or organized the wrong way for the task at hand, it will not prevail in war. In a crisis it may be even less useful, either failing to deter if its nation appears irresolute (France in 1939) or triggering more opposition from terrified neighbors (Germany in 1890–1914). Historical theorizing aside, reliance on a big army alone is foiled by simple arithmetic. No great power can ever field enough soldiers and weapons to meet every conceivable crisis without spending so much as to undermine its economy and society, in the end destroying the very security it desired. Put another way, a country can come close to having enough force to protect all its interests only if it remains perpetually on a war footing. The Soviet Union came closer to doing this than any other modern state in peacetime. Fearing the overwhelming power and wealth of the United States and its allies, and believing that real reconciliation with the West was impossible, the Soviet leaders spent at least four times as much of their GNP[13] on the military than did the United States, with catastrophic results.

While the Soviet Union failed rather spectacularly, its main adversary survived, but not just because of its preponderance of force. The United States was militarily far stronger at the time of the Vietnam War than at the time the Korean War broke out, yet it won the latter and lost the former. (In some respects, the United States faced stronger opposition in Korea than in Vietnam as well, given the participation of Chinese divisions and Soviet proximity.) True, in Korea the United States had a

---

13. It is impossible to be more precise because estimates of Soviet-era GNP are highly variable. In general, they continue to fall, with one recent estimate putting it at less than a seventh of U.S. GNP (a figure I am not ready to accept). If this calculation were generally accepted, the Soviet GNP share for military spending would be about eight times that of the United States.

number of advantages, as compared with Vietnam. The geography was more favorable, local support was much stronger, the quality of generalship was high. That is, of course, precisely the point: Two of the three advantages listed above had nothing to do with quantity or quality of armed force. America had to relearn a lesson learned by many other nations, that being prepared includes a whole range of activities, including

- military force deployment, ensuring that force can be threatened or projected when and where needed.
- risk reduction, whether by withdrawal or lowering of profile, to avoid a multiplicity of crises.
- economic strategy, maintaining economic health and ensuring the security of natural resources.
- politics, the building of domestic support and unity.
- diplomacy, including relationship with foreign governments and foreign peoples.

These things are necessary because a quantitative military advantage is useful primarily at the beginning of a conflict, while survival in war means winning the last battle, not the first. By the same token, crisis survival means success (if only extrication) at the end of the crisis, not the speed with which you can react at the beginning.

The difference between survival and failure in crisis depends on whether preparations were made with the above point in mind. Preparations need to be comprehensive, including political and economic contingencies, as well as the more obvious military variety. Preparations need to be made with long-term problems in mind, not with gaining a momentary, transitory advantage when the crisis begins. Preparations must allow for errors and failures, including the inability to avert war. War preparations must include steps for long-term survival and consideration of how to extricate a country from a war without achieving total victory or suffering total defeat. Extrication from war is the most difficult and delicate task any government can attempt, and it has rarely been done successfully, especially given the emotional tides that rage with such power when the bloodletting has begun.

The inherent difficulty of extrication was overlooked in Vietnam. The flounderings of the American government in the war's later years should perhaps be judged less harshly. Examples of successful extrication are rare. Nations usually wish to leave a conflict when they are losing, which is also the point at which their adversaries are least likely to let them leave. Examples of nations leaving wars without achieving victory or suffering defeat become rarer in recent history. In modern history, Frederick the Great of Prussia extricated himself from the Seven Years' War (1756–1763) only because the new ruler of victorious enemy Russia, Peter III, unilaterally withdrew (and lest the latter action be viewed as a successful extrication, Peter was strangled six months later). The United States successfully withdrew from the War of 1812 because its adversary, Britain, had achieved its goals—without appearing as a clear victor. The United States completed its withdrawal from Vietnam after an apparent tactical air victory (although the extent of this victory has been disputed).

Extrication throughout the history of warfare has been difficult because a request for negotiation signals weakness and encourages the enemy. In the twentieth century, however, another change took place that further complicated extrication: the continuous nature of warfare. Until the late nineteenth century, wars consisted of a series of campaigns separated by periods of supply and casualty replacements, not to mention winter quarters. This gave governments breathing space in which to contemplate the situation. This no longer exists. In World War I, armies were for the first time in contact with each other for years, not days. This complicated extrication by adding a new tactical dimension of disengagement, as well as a psychological one of contemplating withdrawal while the enemy was in sight. This affected people many miles from the front because any withdrawal would lead to occupation of more territory. In addition, a public deluged by constant war news develops a mentality of struggle in which everything increasingly becomes devoted to victory at the front. The desire for extrication disappears.

Taking the big-picture approach to crisis and war preparation is not new. Strategists from ancient to modern times have understood the need to consider all aspects of the national character before deciding what to do. As the American national security establishment has become more professionalized, however, a tendency has developed to take inherent American strengths as a given and to proceed with strategic planning as an external process, looking outward toward the enemy without looking inward toward the nation's politics and economics. Hence Vietnam, which resulted in deep national wounds that have never completely healed.

To be fair, the problem—and the occasional failure to solve it—is not new. The Assyrian empire exploited and overtaxed its subjects to support its enormous military machine. When Babylon attacked (626–612 B.C.), those subjects, far from helping Assyria, rose and destroyed it. Rome, on the other hand, survived the threat from Carthage (264–146 B.C.) because its political system was strong enough to weather defeats (although Roman society emerged from the wars vastly changed). Persia was less lucky; the defeats it suffered at the hands of the Macedonian Alexander the Great (334–331 B.C.) led to the empire's complete collapse and destruction. While Spain's justly famed soldiers and sailors made it the pre-eminent European state in the sixteenth century, its overreliance on their skill reduced Spain to a second-rate power by the seventeenth century. France twice relied on military force for its empire-building (1689–1714, 1799–1815) and twice endured ultimate humiliation. Germany's experience in the two world wars has been recounted too many times to go into detail here, but its lack of preparations was at times breathtaking. In World War I, Germany had stockpiled only enough explosives for six months and might have collapsed except for the fortuitous scientific discovery of how to manufacture explosives without nitrates (which could not be imported after the war began). Germany was well into World War II before it maximized military production. Before World War II, France's military preparations were extensive, but morale was so poor that the country was impotent during the six major prewar crises of 1935–1938[14] and, ultimately, in the war itself.

America's Cold War experience at first looks like solid support for the idea of crisis/war survival through preparation. The military and foreign policy establishment that became entrenched in the early years of the Cold War was enormous and had no peacetime parallel in American history. A closer look changes the picture somewhat. Undoubtedly this helped America defeat the forces of Stalinism. Unfortunately, the world was changing in many other ways as well, and as American attention was focused on the Soviet Union and its allies, the establishment was less successful in coping with, or even understanding, these other changes. For example, one of the most powerful forces in the post-World War II world was Third World nationalism. As a former colony itself, the United

---

14. These were German rearmament (1935), the Italian invasion of Ethiopia (1935), German reoccupation of the Rhineland (1936), the Spanish Civil War (1936), Germany's occupation of Austria (1936), and the Sudetenland (Munich) crisis (1938).

States might have been expected to understand, and possible sympathize with, these movements. It did neither. Nationalist revolutionaries were classified according to American Cold War perceptions, with little regard for the reasons that caused those revolutionaries to revolt in the first place. Cultural love for conspiracy theories merged with Cold War paranoia to produce a world view that the rest of the world often found perplexing, if not bizarre.

This outlook resonated poorly in Europe, where even the pro-American element (more numerous than many Americans realize) became exasperated with American oversimplifications and aggressive rhetoric. The European outlook on the Cold War was subtly but substantially different from that of America. Europeans had endured infinitely more destruction in modern war than Americans. Europe would also be a battlefield if the Cold War became hot. More important, however, Europeans were not experiencing anything new by living next door to an enemy; they had endured this throughout most of European history. Hence, a new mindset was essentially unnecessary, and the paranoia approach was regarded as particularly irrelevant. Finally, Europeans knew more about Soviet Russia than Americans did, partly due to proximity, partly because of better knowledge of Russian history and culture. A giant Russian bear blundering about Eurasia was new and frightening to an American, but ancient history to the Germans or the French. Nevertheless, American military preparations were welcomed in Europe.

These preparations—many undertaken during, not before, the Cold War—were certainly impressive. The military retained a peacetime strength that had no parallel in American history. While the post-World War II demobilization was very fast, the remaining military strength was still some seven times larger than during any other peacetime. An independent Air Force was born, soon to consume three-fifths of the annual defense budget. The Central Intelligence Agency and National Security Agency were created. A single Defense Department and a National Security Council were organized to coordinate this vast and growing crisis-warfare system. The early 1960s saw rapid growth in the size of the military (which passed the 3 million mark during the Vietnam War) and greatly increased spending on the space race, which, NASA public relations notwithstanding, had a clearly military character. The United States Information Agency was created to say that we were good, and the Peace Corps was organized to prove it.

How well did these massive preparations work, and are there lessons for the future in that assessment? As suggested above, the results of the assessment will depend somewhat on the perspective from which it is performed. From a "pure Cold War" view (i.e., confrontation with the Soviet Union), we can be reasonably satisfied without being smug or complacent, concerning the three main types of confrontation: The propaganda war, the military confrontation, and the political struggle.

THE PROPAGANDA WAR

First, the United States never really lost the global propaganda war, and, given our ability to make ourselves unpopular in many different places, that was no small achievement. To be sure, some of the credit must go to the Soviet Union. The Berlin Blockade (1948–1949), the communist coup in Czechoslovakia (1948), the repression of the revolt in Hungary (1956), the invasion of Czechoslovakia (1968), and the shooting down of a Korean passenger jet (1983) were all remarkably helpful to the U.S. government. The United States was frequently criticized by Europeans across the political spectrum, but the trans-Atlantic alliance never collapsed. Propaganda and public opinion were not the only factor here. The western states were and are all capitalist and democratic, and were hardly likely to change sides, no matter what criticisms of the United States emerged. The failure of the Soviet Union to win a clear propaganda victory in the nations of the Southern Hemisphere is more remarkable. Whether the outcome of the propaganda war is attributable to the deliberate efforts of the United States government is debatable. At the least, however, foreign aid, whether government or private, was a cheap way of buying good will and allowed the United States to use its much greater wealth to influence world public opinion.

The Soviet government was in a good position to produce propaganda as well as to seal off knowledge of its domestic problems (up to a point). The underpinnings of this propaganda proved problematical. Much communist propaganda was, of course, communist, emphasizing Marxist-Leninist thought. In the West, the average person proved rather impervious to this line, partly because Europe had variants of Marxist and other socialist thought that were really ahead of its Soviet variant— which nullified some of the propaganda's impact among European intellectuals. Soviet Marxism simply was not the best Marxism around. In the Third World, few states could or did move toward Marxist economics because their societies were—in Marxist terms—not ready for it. The Maoist variant of communism appealed, but this drew its followers toward China—not a development appreciated in Moscow. Many Third World socialist leaders had been educated by Western socialist intellectuals and hence pursued independent lines of thought and action. Finally, Soviet propaganda was dull, hardly snapped up by young people around the world. American magazines, music and newspapers were. This did not guarantee pro-American attitudes—far from it—but it did spread American culture.

THE MILITARY CONFRONTATION

The United States fared well in the military arena of the Cold War, although the ultimate test never came (a success in itself, for both sides). The ability to mobilize and deploy forces, which had been so well tested in World War II, functioned equally well thereafter. The first test of this capacity occurred during the Berlin Blockade when that city had to be resupplied from the air after the Soviet Union cut off most ground access.[15] The Anglo-American air bridge to Berlin demonstrated an immense capacity for moving quantities of materiel (and, therefore, soldiers) and showed that capacity could be sustained for months. The Korean War was a much bigger test, because not only did the U.S. government have to decide on intervention within a matter of days, it also had to rebuild a military establishment still recovering from postwar demobilization. Vietnam saw the concentration of 626,000 troops in Southeast Asia as well as air and naval forces launched from far-flung Pacific bases, and although the war was lost, the deployment itself remains impressive. The other major military confrontations of the Cold War (1962, 1970, 1974) involved nuclear threats and were "waged" without large-scale mobilizations or, in the case of 1962 and 1974, large conventional deployments.

The bottom line is that the United States won one war, lost another, and prevailed in most of the direct confrontations. It's an enviable record, Vietnam notwithstanding. As with the propaganda war, a look behind the superficial record reveals some complexities. The American success in military confrontations was helped by two rather significant advantages. First, the United States had a military edge over the Soviet Union during much of the Cold War. Until the 1960s, the American nuclear arsenal was bigger and more accurate than its Soviet counterpart. By the time

---

15. A minor oversight in the postwar agreements allowed Stalin to cut these routes without in any way violating international law. The blockade was never complete, however.

Soviet atomic technology had closed that gap, America's conventional forces were outpacing the Soviets' although that edge was lost as a result of Vietnam (operating costs of the war ate up the procurement and design budget). Second, the Soviet Union did not display much interest in sending its military far beyond its boundaries. The Soviet Union never really challenged America's global posture in a military way (political challenges were something else). Soviet Russia's deployments to Cuba and Egypt are well known, but beyond that, the external military presence was small (not counting Eastern Europe, of course).

Soviet behavior followed Russian history. Russia historically has been —contradictory as it sounds—an expanding but defensive state. Russia grew not because it wanted to, but because it had to. The Russian state was surrounded by enemies and strove to drive them farther away and to acquire buffer zones. Russia attacked Sweden in 1700 because Sweden's Baltic territories allowed it to threaten Russia's interior. Russia attacked Frederick the Great's Prussia in 1756 because of his aggressiveness and his seizure of ally Austria's province of Silesia in 1740. In the wars of the French Revolution, Russia could easily have demanded all the territory it wanted, as it clearly was the greatest military power in Europe at that point, but it settled for a larger chunk of Poland—and that only to control the Poles! The Soviet state gobbled up borderlands (parts of Finland, Poland, and Rumania) and overran the three Baltic republics (Latvia, Lithuania, and Estonia); the latter conquests were, in Russian eyes, merely a reconquest of lands taken by Peter the Great from Sweden.

This seemingly defensive Soviet posture contributed to an American problem. The United States and its national security establishment had a real problem in the area of enemy identification. To be sure, the Soviet Union was a clear enemy. Yet much of the Cold War revolved around places that were not Soviet-controlled, crises that were not Soviet-caused, and people who were manifestly not Soviet. The Korean War was not Soviet-inspired, although Stalin was closely involved with the detailed planning of the attack. The impetus for the North Korean invasion of South Korea came from the North Koreans. The Vietnam War was even less inspired by the Soviet Union. At first these distinctions were regarded as unimportant because it was assumed that all movements that were communist, or at least looked as if they were communist, were part of a global conspiracy coordinated by Moscow. Unfortunately, this interpretation overlooked the fact that local revolutionaries, including communists, have agendas of their own. U.S. military efforts (including CIA-sponsored expeditions) ran into trouble because in Cuba, Nicaragua, and Vietnam, the enemies had their own reasons for wanting to wage war that were only peripherally related to the Soviet Union and the Cold War.[16]

THE POLITICAL STRUGGLE

Clearly, the Cold War ended with a global defeat for communism, although whether that is a permanent development cannot be foreseen. The United States' victory is ambiguous, however, simply because its political strategy during the Cold War contained many ambiguitics. Throughout the Caribbean basin, the United States used military force and CIA expeditions to attack leftist movements, many of them with no communist ties. In South America, local military dictators were the ally of choice. In Europe, the United States financed friendly political parties on occasion (such as the Italian Christian Democrats). In eastern Asia the Korean and Vietnam wars were fought to contain the expansion of China, although, paradoxically, communist Russia and Vietnam did a better job of that than we did. Nevertheless, the United States emerged from the Cold War with a global network of governments that are, or pretend to be, friendly toward it.

The current dominance of capitalism is also part of this victory. Capitalism is reaching a historical high water mark, slowly becoming accepted (in fact if not in name) in communist China. The capitalist ethos is gaining ground in traditional social democratic states as well. Eastern Europe, has seen the victory of a series of former communist parties, but these do not represent an overt effort to to turn back the clock. In a sense, we now have neocommunism to compete with neoconservatism. This capitalist victory is of strategic benefit to the United States so long as the United States uses its power to stabilize and nurture the capitalist system, something that no powers did in the 1929–1932 Great Depression. Subject to this caveat, the defeat of communism in the Cold War is unambiguous, at least for now.

Whether this was a success gained by skill or good fortune is not the

---

16. It is interesting that the United States' countermoves were not always tied to our confrontation with the Soviet Union. In Cuba and Nicaragua, the United States was merely pursuing its century-old agenda of controlling the Caribbean. This is why we maintain our embargo against Cuba long after the Cold War is over—although that embargo helps keep the hostile Cuban government in power.

point here. The United States government understood that it was involved in a political struggle and attempted to wage it accordingly. This was not, admittedly, the result of brilliant insights, but rather the outgrowth of the World War II experience, when the war was—and was seen as—a struggle against totalitarian governments. In fact, the Soviet Union and its allies were often presented as a new type of Axis, and any Soviet leader would sooner or later be compared to Hitler.

This brings up what was perhaps the biggest weakness of the Cold War national security establishment. Because the national security establishment was organized around a certain world view, and had the resources to attempt to impose that world view on the world, it was less successful in attempting to view the world objectively and to observe trends and problems that were not part of the Cold War. Individuals in the Pentagon or the CIA might be broad-minded, but the bureaucratization of the Cold War created an institutional mindset that could not be overcome from inside. This extended, oddly enough, to analysis of the Soviet Union itself. The national security establishment was so successful in mobilizing the national attitude for the Cold War that it ultimately could not shake off the rather simplistic models of the Soviet Union that prevailed in the national mind. The Soviet Union was portrayed as a revolutionary, communist, expansionist state, long after it had degenerated into a bureaucratic, declining, and insecure empire whose "communism" was little more than a mandatory set of slogans.

More serious was the inability of the national security establishment to cope intelligently with movements and political attitudes abroad that were not communist and had no serious connections with major communist states. Any event that threatened the status quo in areas where America was well established was portrayed, and sometimes honestly seen, as communist. This extended, for example, to the moderately leftist governments of Jacobo Arbenz (Guatemala) and Muhammad Mossadeq (Iran), both of which the United States overthrew, and to the rebellion in the Dominican Republic (1964), during which the American ambassador implied that another Cuba was in the making.[17] The cost of these erroneous generalizations was both short and long term. In the short term,

17. Critics of American foreign policy have suggested that the American government was being dishonest, that it was well known in each of these crises that the revolutionaries were not at all communist, but were merely portrayed as such in order to justify their overthrow. However, Arbenz was actually sympathetic to communism.

the lack of sophisticated and coordinated thinking contributed to the failure in Vietnam, where America was unable to distinguish between communism and nationalism, between the Viet Cong and the North Vietnamese, between North Vietnam and China, and between China and the Soviet Union. In the long run, the tendency to view the world in this oversimplified way cost America an enormous amount of good will that will take years, if not decades, to regain. As the knowledge to avoid these mistakes was internally available, the origins of the problem are institutional, not intellectual:

- Bureaucratization. Institutions organized around a certain belief or a certain function cannot fairly be expected to think or act outside of that belief or function.

- Groupthink. Well studied by political scientists, this is a tendency to think within and only within the assumptions and values held by the members of the group.

- Lack of external criticism. The two above problems result from the intellectual wall that surrounds the security establishment—a wall that faces both ways. Secrecy may protect an organization's functioning but also makes it vulnerable to unarrested internal decay. This is particularly important because many of the national security establishment's organisms work in an atmosphere of secrecy, most of the information known about them is what they choose to release, and they essentially choose who from the "outside" (i.e., consultants) they will communicate with.

These problems, and the others outlined above, indicate that preparations are essential but not by themselves sufficient. That is, even a power that considers itself well prepared by existing measures may find itself faced with problems for which its preparations were insufficient. This is not because the preparations were necessarily wrong. France, for example, was not wrong to rely on the Maginot Line in World War II, but failed to be prepared in other critical areas—most important, air power and mobile forces. The American military was not badly prepared for war when it entered Vietnam, but was not specifically configured for that war and lacked the institutional flexibility to adjust in time. Getting ready for the next crisis and the next war therefore requires preparations to be comprehensive and flexible. To be comprehensive, they must run the full range of military, diplomatic, economic, and political aspects of crisis management and war waging. To be flexible, the institutions that manage crises and conduct wars must contain mechanisms for self-criticism and allow access to the system by people who are not linked to the governing establishment in any way. These outsiders can think and criticize "outside the box," that is, without the intellectual constraints that develop in any group to make members conform to group values and ideas.

Of course, it is easier to make these generalizations than to translate them into specific proposals, or to do so without making exaggerated guarantees about their prospective success. Specifics will be discussed in Chapter 7. At this point, I offer a four-category general proposal for judging our level of preparedness and the validity of future proposals. Getting ready means being prepared in the four following areas:

The Military

Response. How rapidly can the military be mobilized for crises, and how far away?

Sustain. How long can military operations, or even a mobilized status, be maintained?

This issue is raised by concerns that the United States, because of its all-volunteer army and high sensitivity to casualties, has the world's ultimate short war capacity. This has both a quantitative and a psychological dimension. A small military establishment will lose its highly trained and skilled personnel and have to replace them with less skilled troops, who will less effective and killed more rapidly. More subtle is the public sensitivity to casualties, laudably humane but impossible during a lengthy conflict. The national regenerative capacity would be low, because shock over casualties would reduce the willingness to fight and hold on, come what may, in the manner demonstrated by the French in World War I. In 1916 Marshal P. Petain spoke the famous words, "Ils ne passeront pas" (they shall not pass), when Germany attacked at Verdun. Such an attitude, oblivious of cost, is necessary to prevail in a long war.

Threat. To what extent can the military be used to support diplomacy through the intelligent use of threats?

Friends

Alliances. Are workable alliances in place to cover military, political, and economic weaknesses in the event of a crisis?

Foreign aid. Is foreign aid being directed as a tool of foreign policy? Is it effective (in the sense that although one cannot buy friends, one can certainly rent them)? Does the public understand that this is in fact what foreign aid accomplishes?

The United States is not new to this, as it both received foreign aid at a critical time (Revolutionary War) and used foreign aid intensively in major modern wars. In World War II, the huge Lend-Lease Program provided a relatively low-cost way for the United States to bring its economic supremacy to bear on the battlefield.

Risk Reduction

Imports. Has the country reduced as much as possible its raw material imports from regions particularly vulnerable to crisis, which might force our involvement on unfavorable terms?

It has been suggested that Iraq might have had a nuclear bomb by 1992. The next Persian Gulf war will create a much less favorable situation for intervening Western powers.

Hot spots. Has the government intelligently identified the places where confrontation is highly likely, and considered removing or reducing our presence when this is strategically beneficial?

Visible American pressure on Iran only increases that country's hostility and paranoia and may actually increase the risks of terrorism and war. Pressure on Fidel Castro only helps keep him in power.

Warm spots. Is the government sensitive to the presence of revolutionary forces in areas of strategic interest, as revolutions are the ultimate peace destroyers?

Decision Making

Bipartisanship. As severe political differences by definition make long-range planning impossible, is there a policy that both parties can at least accept?

Centralization. Is the decision-making apparatus sufficiently centralized so as to discourage (and perhaps punish) bureaucratic infighting?

Flexibility. Does the decision-making system take change into account, and is it organized to receive outside criticism?

Freedom of action. Do our military and foreign policies consider the need to maintain freedom of action—the ability to maximize one's choices, have as much choice as possible about entering a crisis or war, and retain an ability to leave it?

It is to this last point, which is both fascinating and difficult, that we now turn our attention.

4

THE REAL FREEDOM

The defeats of history's most notorious aggressors are usually attributed to their having overextended themselves. For example, Napoleon waged war simultaneously in Spain and Russia, while Hitler invaded Soviet Russia before resolving his struggle against Britain. Overextension alone, however, cannot fully explain these defeats. Other conquerors, such as Genghis Khan (and even Franklin D. Roosevelt) have taken on as many opponents and prevailed. The success of the great Mongolian and his heirs illustrates why some nations have prevailed and others failed. Despite waging war against countless opponents in Asia, the Middle East, and Europe, the Mongols always retained the initiative, attacked when it suited them, and disengaged when necessary. In other words, they retained their freedom of action.

That they did so despite near-simultaneous wars against widely spaced opponents is all the more remarkable. There were several things that the Mongols had going for them. They had tactical superiority over all their adversaries. This was the last age (twelfth through fifteenth centuries) that so-called "nomadic" warriors could best those from "civilized" nations on a regular basis. Since ancient times, the lightly armed, fast-moving mounted nomadic fighters had proved an elusive target for their better armed and organized, but slower, adversaries. Add to this the formidable organizational skills of Genghis Khan and the Mongols were well nigh invincible. Their speed also enabled the Mongols to withdraw and fight at times and places of their choosing. Finally, the Mongols had a huge geographical advantage: No one could easily invade their homelands. The distances were too great, and the Turkic-Mongol settlements too scattered and sparse, for any adversary to go on the offensive. A large attacking force would have run out of supplies, while a small one would have been surrounded and slaughtered. Unless the next world war reduces humanity to a semi-nomadic state, there are few lessons here, except the inherent advantage conferred by maintaining freedom of action. On the other hand, failure to maintain freedom of action has cost many countries dearly throughout history, as will be demonstrated in this chapter.

Freedom of action is perhaps best understood instinctively rather than through linguistics, especially since it can mean different things in different settings. A simple but straightforward definition is: Freedom of action exists whenever you can make a legitimate choice that is not forced on you, either by circumstances or by an adversary. ("Legitimate" means any choice that advances the national interest and is neither absurd nor suicidal.) This definition is equally applicable to crises and to wars; it is precisely the absence of freedom of action that has forced nations into war even when they had no strong wish to engage. Conversely, war can deprive a country of freedom of action tactically and strategically. On the tactical level, freedom of action is lost if all one's forces are engaged by the enemy or if no means remain to strike at that enemy. Strategically, freedom of action is lost when a country can neither "win" (however defined) a war nor make a graceful exit from it.

The latter point will probably resonate with American readers familiar with the Vietnam War, commonly described as a quagmire. How could it be, thought many Americans, that the world's most powerful and wealthiest country, with a military establishment second to none, found itself unable to win? A partial answer, of course, is that a preponderance of firepower or wealth has never automatically guaranteed victory; actually, nothing has. The truth in Vietnam was much more complicated, however. "Fighting to win" was not practical, certainly not by 1968. By that time domestic opposition to the war was strong, public cynicism about the conduct of the war was rampant, the government and the military had provided no clear strategy, and the Tet Offensive proved that the enemy was not nearly as close to defeat (if at all) as the administration had claimed. There was little agreement about what would constitute a victory, who the real enemies were, and how much more this country was willing to sacrifice to achieve its goals. There was, in fact, little clarity about what those goals were; as many as twenty-five goals have been identified. Whom were we fighting? Choices included "global communism," North Vietnam, the Viet Cong, nationalist revolutionaries, or some combination thereof. Why were our opponents fighting? Again, explanations range from agitation by servants of global communism to a desire for land reform in Vietnam. What were we fighting for? Choices included the containment of communism, the independence of South Vietnam, Southeast Asian natural resources, proving our resolve to the world, defending democracy (not that it existed to defend) and so on. With so much disagreement and confusion, victory was a meaningless word. In strictly military terms, the United States could stay in Southeast Asia as long as it wanted to, and could even overrun other Southeast Asian states if necessary; but none of these would bring the war to an end, none would guarantee the survival of South Vietnam for even a decent interval, and all could have involved costs beyond what the country was willing to pay. The public desired victory but demanded an end to the casualties. In such a situation, pulling out was the only remaining option.

As it happened, pulling out was also impossible. Vietnam, by itself, did not appear terribly important to America's strategic position. Unfortunately, by committing so much effort to the conflict, America had signaled to the world that Vietnam *was* important, so that withdrawal would signal a major weakening of our strategic position (whether it was or not). By the time that Richard Nixon became president, there were no good options (a lack of freedom of action), and a phased withdrawal was executed to salvage some respectability from the fiasco. Until that withdrawal was completed (1973), the United States was doomed to stay at war, unable to control the war's tempo, for eight long years.

It was, in fact, the longest major war in American history; only the war against the Seminole Indians in 1835–1843 matched Vietnam in length. At least that conflict produced a victory for the United States, but one that was unfortunately ignored during Vietnam. The American goals against the Seminoles were perfectly clear: submission and exportation. There was never any question of "why" (on either side). The resources needed to defeat the guerrilla-style Seminole methods were enormous, requiring at one point an American numerical superiority of forty to one. Even then, the defeat of the Seminoles required trickery to capture their most famous leader, Osceola. (The defeat of the Seminoles bears an uncanny resemblance to the Soviet defeat of the Tambov peasant rebellion in 1921–1922.) The Seminole war involved counterinsurgency and conventional warfare in a subtropical setting. The United States could win such a war.

What went wrong in Vietnam wasn't the length of the war. True, public approval can start to disintegrate over time. General George Marshall, World War II army chief of staff and later secretary of state, once opined that a democracy could not win a Seven Years' War (referring to a major war of the eighteenth century). America, however, had the resources to fight longer (most of the war's costs were borne by the Vietnamese, after all). Neither were the losses alone the problem. While American deaths were slightly higher than in the Korean War, they were only half those of World War I, a seventh of those of World War II, a tenth of the Civil War's, and maybe a twentieth of the losses suffered by the various Vietnamese armies. Nor can failure be blamed on a lack of commitment, at least in military terms. By 1968, the United States had deployed 626,000 American personnel in and around Southeast Asia, and more firepower was poured into Vietnam than was used in World War II.

The reasons for failure lay more in the background. Not only were goals unclear and the enemy unidentified, but planning was mediocre and public support was never mobilized. The military was organized and equipped to wage war against Soviet Russia on the northern plain of Europe, not the jungles of Vietnam. The Johnson administration did not want to mobilize public enthusiasm for the war in Asia for fear of undermining its domestic programs. Superficially, this was a peculiar decision, contrasting oddly with Roosevelt's complete commitment of World War II. Johnson, however, was badly advised by Defense Secretary Robert McNamara and others, who believed that the war could be fought as a technology-based sideshow that did not require the traditional outpouring of public support (McNamara had a deep contempt for tradition anyway).

In other words, the United States was not prepared. This is one of the few things that the war's many critics appear to agree on. But if the United States did not prepare well for Vietnam, why could not this defect be remedied later? America would hardly have been the first country to have won a war after a bad start. It comes down to this: Failure to prepare properly can cost a nation its freedom of action.

Freedom of action exists only when choice is present. Again, this means that, in virtually any situation, a government can make decisions that are not forced on it by circumstances or by an adversary. Freedom of action no longer exists if all choices are forced. Freedom of action tends to decline in the midst of crisis or war. In a sense, this is inevitable.

Absent a crisis or war, a government has countless options (including initiation of a conflict). Once a crisis or war is under way, options that do not relate to the particular situation or adversary are obsolete. Unfortunately, this decrease of freedom of action has some rather ominous results. As choices disappear, a nation's options may be reduced to only three: Escalation, withdrawal, or stagnation (letting things continue as they are). The last option probably sounds suspiciously like Vietnam-style "quagmire," and it is. Escalation is particularly dangerous in this context because it occurs more out of desperation than because of any carefully planned strategy. Withdrawal, on the other hand, is fraught with political and technical difficulties. Not for nothing did Germany's greatest general of the nineteenth century, Helmuth von Moltke (victor in three wars between 1864 and 1871) consider retreat the most dangerous maneuver.

The conduct of retreats is such an unpopular topic in military circles that the term does not even get a mention in current U.S. Army doctrine. This is unfortunate, because retreat is absolutely essential for regaining freedom of action. Tactically and strategically, the engagement with an enemy must be temporarily broken before a new operation can begin. This is a relatively modern problem. As late as the Franco-Prussian War (1870–1871) it was still common for armies to engage, battle, and then lose contact for a time as the bested side withdrew. The reasons for such frequent disengagements are straightforward. The defeated and victorious armies needed to regroup, incorporate new recruits, and wait for supplies to catch up with their needs. In the twentieth century, however, warfare took a different tack. Armies were now large and well supplied enough that they could engage in continuous warfare, best exemplified by the trench deadlock of 1914–1918 in World War I. In such circumstances, the term "battle," implying a meeting, a fight, and an end, lost its traditional meaning. Armies could no longer withdraw to regroup (and think things over) because the enemy would pursue with speed and energy unknown in a previous age. This had been made possible by a combination of motorized transport and mass production, which allowed armies to maintain a tempo of battle that, during the "good old days," would have consumed the supply of soldiers and munitions in a matter of hours.

This technological and industrial change had profound consequences. Tactical freedom of action seemed lost. Doctrine and technology eventually restored armies' freedom of movement and therefore some of their freedom of action. The doctrine concerned the use of large mobile formations supported by air power, while the technology was the ground attack aircraft, the fast tank, and motorized and armored infantry. But these improvements could not solve certain underlying problems. The methods described above solved half of the World War I conundrum: how to attack. They did not deal with the dilemma of retreat. If anything, they made it more difficult. Casualties during retreats were always high in warfare, but even more so in our era. The Soviet general staff, for example, discovered during World War II that attacking formations suffered lighter losses than those attempting to withdraw. Retreating formations in 1815 suffered mostly from enemy cavalry pursuit, while the retreating soldier of the 1990s can be pursued by an awesome array of soldiers and weapons—and in contrast to the past, the attackers can probably overtake the retreating force.

Yet regaining freedom of action is the most important thing that a national security establishment can study, because it may be the only way to ensure survival if a crisis or conflict takes an unfortunate and unforeseen path. Tactics is not the main problem. The Soviet Union's Red Army recovered from its retreat in 1941. Britain managed to save its withdrawing army during Hitler's sweep across Western Europe. Saddam Hussein's army survived its debacle in 1991 by means of a concealed retreat of a large percentage of its soldiers. Aerial bombardments, "covering fire," and various ways of misleading the adversary can allow a "safe" retreat, and the recapture of tactical freedom of action. At the strategic level, however, attempts to regain freedom of action through withdrawal cause major problems in politics and national morale. In fact, withdrawal is only "chosen" as an even more desperate step than escalation, which is usually preferred; it carries fewer political risks and does less harm to a nation's "image of power"—its most valuable and least measurable strategic asset.

If escalation is the preferred choice when faced with the escalation/withdrawal/stagnation conundrum, why have governments not sought creative alternatives rather than risking an approach (escalation) that can result in total destruction, especially in the nuclear age? If there is a perception of few (or no) choices, an attitude that "we have no choice" permeates the government, something well documented and studied by political scientists. Presumably the adversary's government will have the same feeling. The result is a continuous series of escalations that can easily culminate in world war and destruction of one or both combatants.

This is not just theory. The issue of freedom of action was first discussed extensively by Ferdinand Foch, the Frenchman who commanded all Allied troops (Americans included) in the final years of World War I. This historically shattering war, regarded by historians as the true beginning of the twentieth century, showed the loss of freedom of action in the prewar crisis and the actual war. In the summer of 1914, the major European states either lacked or voluntarily abandoned their freedom of action. The most bizarre example of this was Germany, which based its actions on a single war plan that, in turn, dictated all political, diplomatic, and military actions. The war produced the most notorious battlefield example of loss of freedom of action that history has ever seen. For fifty months, the opposing armies on the Western Front were so tightly locked in bloody trench warfare that they could neither advance nor retreat, and the conflict became a metaphor for futility. By the war's last year, the opposing alliances were scraping bottom in search of new troops. America, a late entrant, had a couple of million draftees to commit to the struggle. This not only gave America's allies a greater numerical edge, it also restored their freedom of action—and they won.

This demonstrates, in a very crude and common-sense way, how freedom of action works in practice. Obviously, an army that retains a usable reserve of soldiers and firepower will probably win over an opponent who has been forced to throw in everything. This principle should not be taken too far. It could too easily be misused to hold back too many troops in a crisis, giving the enemy a tactical advantage on the battlefield. Nevertheless, World War I is hardly the only case in which the side with the most (if limited) freedom of action won. In World War II, the losing powers lost their freedom of action in the Pacific and Europe. By late 1942, the Axis forces were fully committed. Germany and Japan had no freedom of action left. The United Nations allies, however, still had reserves, available industrial production, etc., and won the war.

The key to understanding the above is the word "usable." A reserve of firepower, manpower and industrial production is usable only if it can be applied, with positive results and without excessive cost, in the crisis or war at hand. During much of the Cold War, the United States and its allies relied on the atomic bomb to bolster their strategic situation. Technically, the bomb was the ultimate in reserve firepower; it could be sent anywhere, anytime to eliminate an adversary. But did its existence improve freedom of action? Not necessarily. Nuclear weapons are hideously destructive but not strategically effective. In a confrontation with a nuclear power like the Soviet Union (as it then was), use of the bomb could invite instant retaliation. In other words, the result of its use might be momentarily positive, but the cost would be much too high. In a smaller conflict, the bomb might destroy the very people we claimed to defend or liberate (for example, Vietnam), or it might destroy the very reserves we wished to safeguard (for example, the gulf war). The of the bomb might not immediately lead to excessive costs, but it would not produce positive results.

The bomb, then, lacks utility and its firepower gives policymakers a false sense of freedom of action. In a crisis, its existence gives them a chance to do something when it might be better to do nothing or to look for a creative alternative. In other words, policymakers might rely on the bomb, and that might make its use more likely. This problem is precisely why President John F. Kennedy embarked on an ambitious expansion of non-nuclear forces. Does this render the bomb useless in terms of freedom of action? Surprisingly, no. The bomb may not enhance one's own freedom of action, but it does reduce the potential adversary's—especially one not in possession of nuclear weapons. The reverse of the freedom of action problem is that of limiting the opponent's freedom of action—although strategists since Sun Tzu[18] have postulated that it is not necessarily wise to take away all of the enemy's options. By the same token, complete freedom of action in the hands of an irresponsible or incompetent leadership is dangerous. The existence of nuclear weaponry does limit some of the more extremely aggressive options, and this is not a bad thing.

The threat of nuclear warfare hung ominously above the Korean peninsula in 1950–1953, as the war there directly involved one nuclear power (the United States) and was fought on the doorstep of another (the Soviet Union) which also participated indirectly. The United States sought to improve its freedom of action through nuclear means, by overtly shipping a nuclear cannon ("Atomic Annie") to Korea. The threat was intended to permit withdrawal (by forcing negotiations to a meaningful conclusion), not escalation. The issue of freedom of action hung over all the war's participants. Douglas MacArthur, American commander in Korea at the beginning of the Korean War, was fired because of his strident demands for an attack on China, a move that might have

---

18. Estimates when he lived range from 500 B.C. to the fourth century B.C. His name is sometimes transliterated as Sun Zi, Zun Zi, or Sun Si.

succeeded but would have required years of costly warfare in Asia—an endeavor that would have stretched even America's resources, divided the country politically, and cost it its freedom of action.

Defenders of MacArthur may argue this point, suggesting that his strategy would have led to a reunified Korea and hence avoided the current tensions on the peninsula—a kind of long-term regaining of freedom of action. Korea might indeed have been reunified. Whether the United States or one of its adversaries would have accomplished this is another question. MacArthur's strategy, however, would have required a commitment to fight World War III—and even if the country had been ready for that (doubtful) and our allies would have supported it (more doubtful), the loss of freedom of action would have been total.

Instead of fighting a regional Asian conflict, the United States would have become directly involved in conflict inside China. The number of soldiers required would have far exceeded the active and reserve forces available (although there were, of course, many World War II veterans around). Mobilization would have followed. The economy would once again have gone on a war footing. In other words, the United States would have had to commit its military and economy to a near-total war. Whether it would have become global is more difficult to say. In MacArthur's defense, the Soviet Union would probably have stayed out. Stalin was initially not concerned about North Korea's conquest, although he did ask China to send ground troops to help. The risk, however, would have been tremendous, and America would have had to prepare for a potential Soviet entry—thereby limiting our options further, and creating a situation in which freedom of action disappeared. This happened in Vietnam.

"Atomic Annie" could not rescue America in Vietnam. Paradoxically, because no great-power opponent was militarily present in Vietnam, the nuclear threat was not meaningful. A nuclear slaughter of millions of North Vietnamese would have destroyed America's foreign policy everywhere else, and rightly so. The United States had assembled a number of alliances as well as numerous secret "understandings" for waging the Cold War. These would have collapsed. Every Third World ally of note would have cut its ties with the United States before the dust from the bombing settled. There has always been the entirely erroneous suggestion that the United States would use the atomic bomb only against non-Caucasian races, and an atomic bombing of Vietnam would have given this view great credence in non-Caucasian nations. The condemnations of such an action would have been universal in the Third World, especially because many of its inhabitants saw Vietnam in terms of their own anti-colonial struggles.

The situation would have been almost as bad in Europe. The Left would have viewed it with horror, while even the pro-American Right would condemn the action as incompetence—since the bomb's use would prove that America had no other means left of winning the war. The survival of NATO, the most important alliance, would have been doubtful. The bottom line is that the Cold War was a "hearts and minds" conflict that required taking the moral high ground—at least publicly—and that would have no longer been possible.

This discussion of atomic weapons and Vietnam might seem a bit theoretical, unless we recall that in 1954 there was a serious proposal to use atomic bombs to rescue the French army at Dien Bien Phu. Even if the idea never resurfaced, the above considerations also limited the chances of using even more massive firepower than was used or, for that matter, expanding the war geographically. Consider the trouble Nixon experienced with his limited incursion into Cambodia. Since that was not possible, even more firepower and atomic technology were ruled out by the fact that the war was mostly fought on the soil of an ally. Hence, the only way to win appeared to be through a long and bitter ground war, but this could only be achieved by continuously expanding the size of the American army in Vietnam. The request by Generals Wheeler and Westmoreland for more troops in 1968 was a crude attempt to increase tactical freedom of action but merely precipitated the departure of an honest soldier whose talents were mismatched with the situation.

Expanding the ground army in Vietnam was not a serious option beyond a certain point, but the government did discover a solution that superficially produced freedom of action: air strikes. Air strikes have a remained an American favorite ever since because they are low-casualty (for us), high-tech, and give the illusion that they preserve freedom of action while waging war. But it is just an illusion because air strikes can produce just as irrevocable a commitment as ground forces use. Air strikes are highly visible, which will lead to public involvement and demands for further action if the problem is not solved, and will require allies to take positions for or against the operation. The country attacked with air strikes may consider the action just as intrusive as a ground invasion, and will look for a way to retaliate. Second, air strikes generate more videos than victories. In each of this century's major wars, air power advocates have promised more than they could deliver. Therefore, air strikes usually have to be followed with other actions for the operation to have any real long-term impact.

High-tech firepower (air strikes, nuclear weapons) cannot, therefore, succeed alone as a means for maintaining freedom of action. With nuclear weapons, the usability problems are overwhelming, and the political consequences can make the freedom of action gained rather fleeting. With air power, there are too few situations in which it alone can be decisive, and a method of war or crisis management that is ineffectual gives a country only the same freedom of action as if nothing had been done at all. Air power is politically attractive and popular, which are two terrible reasons for choosing a strategy or a weapon— terrible, but occasionally necessary.

The maintenance of public support in a crisis or a war is vital. Sometimes it becomes necessary to make a decision that, in a vacuum, looks bad, but in reality furthers the national interest. In 1940, Winston Churchill noticed that there was less and less anti-aircraft fire heard in nighttime London, and was told that the guns were wearing out and hits on German planes were rare. Churchill ordered the firing to resume. The roar of the guns gave Londoners the feeling that they were fighting back, and the maintenance of morale was more important to Churchill than the maintenance of his guns. The same logic applies during a crisis. If public opinion becomes uncertain about a government's decision-making in a crisis, the public may demand congressional investigations, visible successful actions, and so on, all pressuring the government even more to take questionable decisions. In other words, a low-risk choice of action that appeals to the public can be a good thing in the long run, even if it is not technically the ideal decision. The key phrase here is "low risk." Churchill knew that the condition of his anti-aircraft guns probably would not much affect the course of the war. However, a crisis decision made to soothe public concerns, while ignoring the foreign consequences, can be very dangerous indeed.

Another difficulty with nuclear weapons and air strikes is that freedom of action cannot be gained or maintained simply by increasing firepower. If extra firepower preserved freedom of action, greater powers would inevitably defeat smaller ones without undue problems related to becoming entangled (the "quagmire" effect). More important, if freedom of action was related to the size of the gun, great powers should always have more freedom of action than smaller ones. The history of modern warfare and crises demonstrates that the first statement is rarely true, while the second is simply false. At first glance, this seems odd. After all, barring unusual circumstances, a greater power should be able to overwhelm a smaller one. There are always, however, unusual circumstances;

- The smaller power may have allies, providing direct military assistance or at least enough backing to discourage the greater power from embarking on a war of total destruction (for fear of bringing in the allies).
- The smaller power may wage war in places that are remote or that contain terrain that nullifies some of the greater power's advantages.
- The smaller power may fight in ways designed to compensate for the great power's military superiority.
- The great power may have other commitments that prevent it from using all its military resources against the smaller power.
- The great power may not be able to use all its firepower against the smaller power for political and diplomatic reasons.

All these circumstances occurred in Vietnam. The Vietnamese adversaries received backing from China and the Soviet Union (and sympathy from others) and fought the war on their terms, while the United States had to reserve much of its strength for other contingencies. America could not infinitely escalate the conflict because of the devastating effect this could have on our own alliances, on the relationship with our major rival, and on domestic political opinion. The country with the greatest amount of firepower in history could neither win nor make a dignified exit. The smaller combatant had more freedom of action than the larger.

Vietnam was not unique in this regard. Many an invasion of a small power has caused fatal complications for the larger. In World War I, Germany invaded and quickly overran Belgium, but in the process gained a larger enemy (Britain) and lost much of its freedom of action, particularly at sea. In World War II, Germany invaded and overran Poland, but thereby gained two new enemies (Britain and France) and, more significant, a common border with its eventual deadly enemy, the Soviet Union. In 1950 North Korea invaded a much weaker South Korea, but quickly found itself opposed by the United States and its allies. The tables turned, however. The United States overran most of North Korea, but China entered the war and threw 300,000 soldiers across the border to stop the U.S. advance (it worked). In a matter of months, the United States, China, and North Korea had lost their freedom of action.

Only the Soviet Union did well in this situation, mainly because of Stalin's flexibility, use of surrogates, and calm responses.[19] Stalin probably did assume in 1950 that the United States did not care about Korea. Secretary of State Dean Acheson had left Korea out of a speech in which he describe the American "defensive perimeter" in the Pacific. Soviet Foreign Minister Vyacheslav Molotov discussed this speech with Chinese communist leader Mao Ze Dong, which makes it all but inevitable that Stalin knew about it. Stalin was trying to make a gain for communism without jeopardizing his position or his freedom of action. He simply allowed North Korean dictator Kim Il Sung to attack, while being closely involved in the planning. When things went awry and an American conquest seemed inevitable, Stalin's reaction was mild. He encouraged a Chinese response, but he privately expressed little concern about an American-dominated Korea. In fact, his response was so mild that it seems almost out of character for the usually paranoid Soviet dictator. Perhaps it best to conclude that Stalin retained his freedom of action by remaining (largely) a nonparticipant. The early military victories led to nothing but loss of freedom of action.

The gulf war provides another highly visible example of this pattern. Saddam Hussein, dictator of Iraq, lost his freedom of action quickly after overrunning Kuwait. Faced with the biggest coalition in the history of the world, he had little alternative but to suffer defeat or accept humiliation. However, it was not Hussein who ultimately suffered the more obvious loss of freedom. There could be no doubt that the U.S./U.N. coalition would defeat Saddam Hussein. The diplomatic and strategic constraints on the United States were so great, however, that it lacked the freedom of action to overrun Iraq and expel the tyrant from Baghdad. Diplomatically, destroying Hussein would destroy the coalition. Strategically, the fall of Hussein could be the end of Iraq, leaving the region dominated by Iran and Syria—not an attractive alternative for the United States.

In essence, the greater power in this war lacked freedom of action precisely because it was a great power. The magnitude of its firepower was both undeniable and unstoppable. The American government, however, had to evaluate every action in terms of its impact on relations with Europe, Russia, China, and the allied Arab states—and even Iran. Hussein faced none of these constraints and was able to move more

---

19. Admittedly, there is disagreement among scholars about his reaction to the U.S./U.N. advance to Inchon.

recklessly than his adversaries. He lost many people (not likely to concern him) and some territory he only held a few months. He survived by retaining his freedom of action almost through the entire crisis—and still does so today, having now outlasted the war by six years and retaining a (weakened) initiative. In fact, survival and victory appear so closely linked (n the sense that the former is oftentimes the most important factor in the latter) that we could conclude that survival requires freedom of action.

This idea can be taken too far, and in American strategic history, it has been. The great temptation in this country is to maintain freedom of action through disengagement or, to put a more traditional way, avoiding entangling alliances. The latter idea comes from George Washington's farewell address, and in his time it made sense—although not for the reason most people assume. Many of the Founding Fathers feared that America's great military weakness would make it vulnerable if it were dragged into a European war. Our later image of America focuses on the frontier, but the country's wealth then lay on its coast, in cities such as Boston, New York, Baltimore, Savannah, Charleston, and, in the following century, Washington and New Orleans. The burning of Washington in the War of 1812 proved the vulnerability of coastal cities (although the others attacked, Baltimore and New Orleans, escaped unscathed). George Washington was not so naive as to ignore connections between countries. The United States had received enormous foreign aid during the Revolutionary War, for example. Washington, however, did not want to be trapped into going to war and wanted to maintain his freedom of action.

His words were heeded, perhaps because they fit nicely with American distrust of foreign countries and foreign affairs, and the country's geographical isolation. Events of this century reinforced American attitudes. In World War I, "entangling alliances" contributed to a war that plunged a civilization into ruin. During the Cold War, however, the United States reversed course and became the greatest alliance-builder in history. American diplomats helped forge the United Nations, the International Monetary Fund, the International Bank for Reconstruction and Development (better known as the World Bank), the General Agreement on Tariffs and Trade, the North Atlantic Treaty Organization, the Central Treaty Organization, the South East Asia Treaty Organization, and a host of others.

What had changed? The Cold War was not regarded as a "peacetime" situation in Washington, and hence traditional concerns about entanglements were swept aside. Furthermore, the United States was the world's greatest power during the Cold War, and hence was developing the entanglements rather than being a victim of them. Pearl Harbor was also a blow to isolationism (although prewar American policy in the Pacific was hardly isolationist). The long-range bomber and intercontinental missile were invented. Now the Cold War is over, and isolationism has regained some strength. Should the United States increase its freedom of action by returning to an isolationist position?

First, even the most valid principle should never be followed blindly, especially where crisis and war are concerned, in which so much is unpredictable because the outcome is determined by unmeasurable vagaries of human emotion. Freedom of action may well be the most important strategic principle, but it does not obliterate all other strategic principles. For example, every country must protect its "vital interests," which, for America, include the flow of natural resources and shielding overseas markets and investments from foreign aggression. Alliances and treaties may be necessary to secure all these.

Second, an American global strategic withdrawal would trigger instability in Europe, the Far East, and the Middle East. The odds against two (let alone three) of these regions remaining peaceful would be astronomical. The result would be multiple crises that the United States might have to enter in order to protect its vital interests. Military resources would be overstretched and the United States would have no treaties or alliances in place to help get the job done. Neither would there be any American troops on location to deter reckless initiatives. For example, the tussles between the two Koreas have been limited because both governments know that certain actions would invite American retaliation of some kind; North Korean recklessness would cause a military reply, while South Korean recklessness could lead to a military withdrawal. Abandonment of Korea would end these constraints on Korean behavior.

Finally, an alliance can sometimes prevent a crisis or even a war. As a result, freedom of action can be enhanced, not reduced, through an alliance. An alliance can secure one strategic flank so that a government may focus its attention on the other. Only the strong alliance with Europe allowed the United States to contest Korea and Vietnam (with mixed results, to be sure). World War II presents the alternative. Britain and France failed to stop Hitler's expansionism (1935–1939) not because of stupidity or cowardice, but because two participants in the previous World War, Russia and America, were now isolated. In fact, American law would have forbidden the French and British even to purchase war-related supplies on the North American market. Entanglements were temporarily avoided, but war was not.

Isolationism as a means for maintaining freedom of action still has some utility, however. Certainly the United States became hopelessly overcommitted during the Cold War and could never have met all its commitments (even with alliances). Isolationists can help bring balance to the strategic picture. There is, however, a far more dangerous idea than isolationism. Freedom of action obviously is designed to maintain the ability to take the initiative. This could lead to the dangerous and false conclusion that the best way to protect freedom of action is to take the military initiative; in other words, attack. Would aggression— initiating crises rather than always responding to them—maintain freedom of action? The answer is yes, but not for long. Having the freedom of action to decide on attack is not the same thing as attacking. In the latter case, freedom of action disappears almost immediately.

Crisis initiators have not fared well in this century. The Austrian Empire initiated the crisis that led to World War I (to be fair, in response to the assassination of its crown prince) and was destroyed. The three Axis powers in World War II, all of which initiated aggression, were destroyed. Khrushchev's decision to place missiles in Cuba ended in a humiliating withdrawal and may have contributed to his removal two years later. Egypt's decision to close the waterway to southern Israel triggered the Six Day War (1967) and Egypt's defeat. North Korea's offensive in 1950 and Saddam Hussein's aggression in 1990 were similarly ill-fated, although both countries (and both dictators) survived. Why have crisis initiators not fared better, despite exercising great, if only momentary, freedom of action?

First, as mentioned earlier, freedom of action disappears quickly once the crisis (or war) has been initiated. Second, a country perceived as aggressive generates opposition. In four of the six examples listed above, the crisis initiators were beaten back by an overwhelming alliance. Third, freedom of action is a valuable asset that can be squandered all too easily by blundering into a conflict.

Fourth, freedom of action is not improved by aggression because policymakers who choose such an action confuse initiative during a crisis with initiating a crisis. These are quite different things. Using freedom of action to take the initiative in the midst of a war or crisis does not automatically increase risk (after all, the crisis is already under way). It is a tactic of proven value that enhances the chances for survival. Using freedom of action to initiate a crisis or war is a catastrophically dangerous tactic because once done, the crisis or war has begun, meaning that freedom of action has been lost. The national fate now rests partly with foreign powers. Such a step makes sense only if the aggressor has absolutely nothing to lose. (This is one reason that diplomats and strategists need to consider Sun Tzu's advice that the adversary should be given a way out, an opportunity to withdraw.) One reason for the different outcomes between initiating a crisis and initiative during a crisis is foreseeability. Once in a war or crisis, a government can make reasonable projections as to whether inaction will lead to disaster, or whether action offers a way out. The government's reasoning may not be correct, but at least some facts are available on which to base the decision. A calculation can be made as to whether the action is going to destroy freedom of action. In fact, using freedom of action to take the initiative in war or crisis is exactly what freedom of action is for. Failure to act could cause the initiative to pass to the adversary, and result in a loss of freedom of action. On the other hand, using freedom of action to create a crisis or start a war would put a government in the reverse situation. Initiative quickly passes from the aggressor to the allies of the victim. Even modern history's most infamous aggressor, Adolf Hitler, held the initiative for only a third of all of world war II. The reason, so richly exemplified in both world wars, is that very little is knowable about the possible flow of a conflict or crisis at the time of its outbreak. Even if the Nazi high command had been better informed about its three major European adversaries, it could not have predicted their actions and policies. Military strength is also notoriously hard to measure before the fighting starts; morale and unit cohesion, for example, cannot really be studied until the shooting starts.

Freedom of action is a valuable tool, but only in the hands of the right user. Obviously, a country must be diplomatically and military prepared and be willing to approach its strategic problems thoughtfully for freedom of action to have any utility. Even more important, however, is the timing of its use. Freedom of action is valuable only if it is used at the right time and in the right context. It will be of no use if it is squandered carelessly. In other words, freedom of action is a valuable asset only if the right decisions are made at the right time.

We now therefore turn our attention to the problem of making "right" decisions.

5

DECIDING

Generations of leaders have looked for a set of rules to guide their decisions, and there has been no shortage of advice. Beginning with the ancient Chinese strategist Sun Tzu, generals, strategists, politicians, and interested observers have tried to distill their thoughts into a set of sayings and ideas that would guide future leaders to "correct" decisions. Such writings were useful but suffered from some inevitable problems. First, the environment has changed. Until the late nineteenth century, communications were slow, and governments had comparatively large amounts of lead time to make decisions. The telegraph and the railway, however, sped up the pace of events and forced leaders to make momentous decisions with no opportunity for reflection on the alternatives or the consequences. The railway made it possible for armies to be mobilized more quickly and to be resupplied without pause. The pace of war had accelerated, and hesitation could mean being overrun. The smaller nations especially felt this. But if the train changed the military frontier, the telegraph entered the mind. By 1914, the gap between diplomatic messages had shrunk to hours—and a failure to answer might be interpreted as hostile.

Second, leaders today have neither the time nor the inclination to study ancient wisdom while facing the threat of annihilation. Chaos theorists might question whether all this ancient wisdom would be of much utility, but surely no one could suggest that ignorance is the best foundation for decision-making. Politicians whose gut instincts have been honed on the domestic battlefield suddenly have to make rapid decisions about crises in far-away places about which they know little, certainly not the cultural complexities to be found anywhere. In other words, the quality of decision-making during a crisis today depends on what has been done before the crisis. If there is no preparation, decisions will be based on panic, political pressures, and gut feelings, none of which may have any relation to the reality of the situation. Survival would depend on luck alone, and the results could be catastrophic.

Historians would be the last to deny that chance has played a role in the outcome of virtually every war and crisis. Luck and chance may not be the best terms to define what is happening when unforeseen events turn the proverbial tide of history. Napoleon realized this exceptionally well and always planned and maneuvered to take advantage of unforeseeable circumstances. During World War II, the United States won the pivotal battle at Midway (1942) because a lieutenant commander, flying beyond the point dictated by fuel supplies, spotted and destroyed three of the four Japanese aircraft carriers. For the United States, this was lucky, but other factors had placed the Japanese fleet in a vulnerable position, not the least being accusations of cowardice aimed at the Japanese commander. This caused Nagumo Chuichi to press on when he should not have done so, and his fear of losing face happened to intersect with Clarence McClusky's wish to fly farther. These two independent decisions happened to intersect at a point in time and space that was catastrophic for Japan. Hitler's massive bombardments of London began as retaliation for a British attack on Berlin, which was a retaliation for a German bombing of the British royal palace, which was an accident caused by deliberate British interference with German navigation equipment. Yet it was the Nazi dictator's aggressiveness that preordained his switch to London, unintentionally saving the Royal Air Force in the process (its bases and formations had suffered heavily up to this point). In one sense, Britain was lucky. In another, the "luck" was the convergence of a series of events and trends that neither side clearly understood at the time. These examples lead to the conclusion that war and crisis survival must take as many factors as possible into account, while retaining the mental and tactical capacity to remain flexible to cope with situations such as those above. Convergence of unforeseen trends can assist survival, but not produce it by itself.

Military establishments, and to a lesser extent, governments, have sought to prevent the above problem by thinking and planning in terms of "worst-case" scenarios. In practice, this meant preparing detailed plans that set out the steps that are to be taken in each contingency. Such plans at least give the writers a comfortable feeling of being prepared for the future. Their effectiveness is another matter. Crises are by definition unpredictable and may outrun all attempts at prediction. The plan may contain fatal and unforeseeable flaws; after all, it cannot be really tested until the moment of action comes. Finally, planning can disturb one of the essential requirements for crisis survival: flexibility. If you lose flexibility, you will be forced to take a series of predetermined decisions —as called for by the plan—even when those decisions are not the best. This happens because, in a crisis, the plan that is already on the table will have a powerful advantage over any proposals made in the midst of crisis. The existing plan is backed by authority and the accumulated, alleged wisdom of a generation of leaders.

The reality is that massive advance plans for crises have a checkered record at best. They should be made, of course, particularly as regards technical matters. The movement of a hundred thousand troops from one continent to another cannot be organized overnight. But as far as the "big picture" goes, detailed advance plans can be as dangerous as they might be helpful. The best-known example of this occurred in 1914, when, on the eve of World War I, virtually every major European power had highly detailed military plans that called for rapid mobilization during a crisis. All armies of the time assumed that delay was more dangerous than risking war. This was an attitude similar to the "use 'em or lose 'em" philosophy of nuclear strategy (better to fire than to risk destruction of one's missiles).

The plans—in particular Germany's—became themselves a major factor in bringing about a war that benefited not a single one of the major participants. The German plan, named the Schlieffen Plan after its author, Alfred von Schlieffen, required Germany to launch an immediate attack on France and Belgium in case of a European war, even though the 1914 crisis began in and was still limited to the eastern side of the continent. The plans were not bad. They mostly accomplished what they were intended to (except for securing the quick victory everyone wanted). The real fallacy was that the plans were out of phase with (if not irrelevant to) the reality of the situation.

The Russian plan contained a notorious technical flaw but, more important, bore no relationship to Russia's inability to supply its armies. The factories and the transport simply weren't there to support an offensive campaign. For strategic reasons, Russia had to attack anyway.

Its plans failed, however, to take the country's economic maladies into account. The Austrians did worse. They attempted to attack two enemies at once, exceeding their command and control mechanisms, as well as their intelligence capability. France's attempt to carry the war to enemy soil was foiled as much by faulty intelligence as the oft-discussed tactical shortcomings of the French army. Even the famed Schlieffen Plan was too big for the German army and too optimistic about the speed at which foot soldiers could walk.

A casual reading of the events of 1914 might lead us to fall into another trap, to assume that World War I-era leaders were simply too aggressive and that the plans would have been acceptable if the great powers had been more cautious. Even if true, it would only be true in 1914. The aggressiveness of the 1914-vintage plans was a mistake for technical military reasons that would cease to apply within two decades. In 1914, the defense had a decided advantage over the offense. Quick-firing artillery, machine guns, and barbed wire had made it difficult for infantry units to close the range with the defense. Technology was not the only factor, however. Armies had simply outgrown their command and control systems. The dimension of time and space in war exceeded anything known before. Field telephones could over time give commanders some contact with the forward units, but that contact was almost impossible to maintain during an attack. Even if the attacking troops reached the defenders' trenches, the attackers would be so completely disorganized that there was no chance of continuing the attack long enough to get through the entire trench system.

When World War II began in 1939, however, the offense had regained the edge over the defense. Documentaries of the period stress the role of technology, but this was only part of the picture. Virtually every weapon of World War II was in use at the end of World War I. Rather, armies had learned (slowly) how to adapt to different styles of war, how to incorporate new technology, and—critically—how to make the attackers less of a target. The broad, mass-infantry assault of World War I, left over from Napoleonic days, was forgotten. An integrated fighting system came into existence, the tempo of attack could be maintained, and the offense had regained the advantage. This was established in May 1940, when Germany secured one of the most one-sided victories in the history of warfare by defeating the French and British armies in two weeks (the French surrendered four weeks later). Tactical aggressiveness paid in World War II. Yet France had not ignored the danger of German invasion (no neighbor of Germany could). The French built a tremendous defensive fortification known as the Maginot Line, which became a metaphor for bad planning. This is not entirely fair, as it was the rest of the French plan that failed, not the Maginot Line itself. All the same, the French and British had a precisely defined plan of war with only one defect: It was out of phase with (if not irrelevant to) the reality of the situation. Neither Allied army had grasped the new superiority of the offense, and each opted for a defensive posture. Both armies were behind the curve in incorporating their technology. The most culpable error, however, was that there was no reserve. This error was based on the assumption that the Nazis would not break through—and if the assumption had been correct, the absence of a reserve would never have been noticed. The Anglo-French strategy also left forces strung out over an exceptionally long front, with France's best mobile army winding up at the extreme left of the line (near Breda, in the Netherlands) where it would have the least influence on the outcome of the fighting. The Anglo-French soldiers were not fools and studied available information carefully, yet their carefully crafted plans failed catastrophically. Poor planning, then, is a defect applicable to both world wars, and there is no reason that it cannot exist in military planning today.

The reality is that, throughout World War II, most actions were based on plans made (and sometimes thrown together) in response to particular crises and contingencies. To take an extreme example, the Soviet Union was thrown into such total chaos by the Nazi invasion in 1941 that it virtually had to reinvent its army, not to mention making completely new plans. It is tempting but wrong to think that planning is really of no help for surviving a crisis, let alone a war. To reject planning altogether ignores the fact that there are at least three types: (1) planning that determines what decisions will be made; (2) planning that determines how decisions will be made; and (3) planning which determines how decisions will be carried out.

Type (3) refers only to what should be technical plans, such as moving the army from one place to another. All countries make such plans. The American military, for example, had written plans before both world wars (although President Woodrow Wilson had the plans written before World War I burned). The value of technical plans is unquestionable—almost. They work perfectly well if they are not allowed to become more than technical plans. Unfortunately, they frequently do, with disturbing results. In 1914, the German war plan was allowed to drive the whole government's decision-making machinery, depriving Germany's leaders of any flexibility and branding Germany as the aggressor. Germans defended the rapid execution of their plan, which dragged Belgium, France, and Britain into the war by pleading "military necessity." Now that phrase is more interesting than it sounds. At the time, it led Germany to be vilified even more, because it sounded like proof that Germany was militaristic and aggressive. In reality, it meant that Germany had allowed its technical military plans—type (3)—to replace and supersede its diplomacy, its national strategy, and so on.

Unfortunately, no nation is immune from such a mistake. In Vietnam, for example, the United States was faced with a complex combination of foes in a battle not so much for territory as for political goals (hearts and minds, stabilizing the pro-U.S. government, etc.). Very little the United States did in Vietnam bore much of a relationship to the nature of the war. Our technical military plans called for victory through firepower—especially air power—and therefore that was the approach used. The weapon chose the strategy, not the other way around. Similarly, nuclear weapons use is governed through the Single Integrated Options Plan (SIOP), which, given the constraints of time in a true nuclear crisis, would become the basis of all decision-making; technical factors relating to the bombs would quickly overpower any real strategic thought. Cruise missiles are our weapon of choice today, not necessarily because they accomplish our strategic goal, but because they happen to be available and can be fired from many sites (and, to be fair, for a political/strategic reason: Their use poses the least risk of almost any weapon).

The other kind of planning we have examined is type (1). This kind of planning is an attempt to create advance certainty in an uncertain world, as well as to cope with the pace with which crises and wars move in our century, which allows too little time for reflection. Soldiers and statesmen have long been aware of the drawbacks of such planning, but it seems safer than risking chaos. As seen above, this safety is largely illusory. One obvious solution was to create a series of contingency advance plans, each to be activated in response to a particular crisis. This does preserve some flexibility, but problems exist even here. First, any crisis will be fitted into one of the contingency plans, even if the facts don't quite fit the assumptions of the original contingency. For example, America's Cold War military strategy assumed that left-wing revolutions and wars resulted from attempts to expand communism, and in particular, the power of the Soviet Union. Yet neither of our two largest Cold War conflicts—Korea and Vietnam—exactly fitted this contingency. The Korean War had more to do with the reckless ambitions of North Korean dictator Kim Il Sung than with the expansionist tendencies of Soviet dictator Josef Stalin who, homicidal psychopath that he was, tended toward caution in international affairs. In Vietnam, most of the war's causes originated inside Vietnam itself. Considering the mistaken assumptions that governed our war effort, we were rather lucky to win one of these conflicts (Korea).

Another problem with contingency plans of the first type is that they are all based on observations and information that may not be accurate. True, information gathering in advance is of inestimable value, and probably better than information that has to be gathered in the midst of a crisis. But knowledge and understanding may have improved, or at least changed, since the plan was written. The writers of the original plan may have had assumptions and ideas not entirely clear to the people reading them during a later crisis. Language changes in subtle ways over time as well. A plan may have faulty basic assumptions, as was true, for example, of German planning in both world wars. In World War I, German leaders sincerely believed that they had to strike quickly because everyone was plotting their destruction. In World War II, Nazi assumptions about racial superiority and inferiority made it impossible to think sensibly at all, and may have contributed to the fatal decision to invade the Soviet Union in 1941. But the most important problem here is that as information and observations are always somewhat inaccurate, rigid plans—type (1)—are doomed to failure. By definition, they cannot adjust to circumstances and bring themselves into phase with reality.

The information that plans are based on is necessarily out of date by the time that they are executed. Updating information does not solve the problem entirely. The intentions of foreign governments can only be hypothesized, because the domestic political pressures on those governments can change rapidly. In wartime, the adversary has a clear interest in keeping information secret, and hence knowledge about the adversary's operations and intentions will be even more uncertain. This phenomenon has been described as the "fog of war." But there is a more subtle reason that the relationship between type (1) plans and the information behind them causes so much trouble. When the plan is prepared, the authors cannot possibly know what type of information is needed. During a crisis, certain facts may be essential for making a decision. When the plan is written, there is no way of knowing what those future facts might be.

This does not mean that planning outside the technical area should be abandoned. If there were no plans, including contingency plans, there would be chaos in the midst of every crisis. Crises and wars have their own momentum, and a large part of surviving such an event is imposing one's will on the situation. To put it another way, crisis management and war survival or victory depend on controlling events, not being controlled by them. The alternative is either chaos or submission to the tide of events. There are two ways to get around the inherent problems of inflexible planning. First, planning can still usefully exist in the form of policy, that is, a set of rules or guidelines according to which decisions in a crisis will be made. A firm and clear general strategy will be used to guide decisions during a crisis.

Such a policy approach to type (1) planning has special benefits for democracies like the United States because it is more difficult for a democratic society to agree to a plan or to change in midstream than it is for an authoritarian regime. This is not because dictators can do anything they like; that is something of a popular myth. But a dictator can change plans and then justify them, while in a democratic society, a lengthy period of debate and even chaos can precede a major shift. This was apparent in Vietnam. As the government blundered from one plan to another, domestic opposition grew—stimulated as much by the obvious incompetence of the leadership as anything else—and this increasingly tied the hands of the government's decision-makers (not that this really mattered, as their decisions tended to be wrong anyway). People who complain about the problems occasioned by this domestic disarray forget that in earlier major wars, the enemy simplified our political problems. In Korea, there was no question in the American mind regarding who the aggressor was. In World War II, Japan settled the issue by bombing the American fleet at Pearl Harbor on December 7, 1941. The situation might have been considerably different if Japan had pursued its other aggressions in the Pacific but had not fired the first shots at American forces. In other words, in Korea and World War II, domestic unity was real, but artificially generated. No country can count on its enemies being so stupid. Ho Chi Minh was wiser; although he did not cause America's domestic Vietnam problems, he certainly did not feel compelled to help us out.

Agreement on policy in advance at least prevents domestic breakdown in crisis. This was shown many times during the Cold War. If you look past the rhetoric and election-year posturing, the Democrats and Republicans were broadly in agreement on American policy and strategy during the Cold War. Conventional wisdom states that this consensus collapsed with Vietnam, but the conventional wisdom here is wrong. Even during the 1980s, as the Cold War entered its final phase, partisan disagreements centered mostly on means, not ends. For example, both parties agreed that it would be a good thing to have a pro-American government in Nicaragua. They disagreed about whether this should be achieved through war or diplomacy. This long near-unanimity is not easy to explain. Its roots lay mostly in the shared experiences of World War II, fear of the Soviet Union, and communist behavior in Eastern and Central Europe in 1945–1949. The result was a remarkable level of stability in American foreign policy—to the point, unfortunately, that thinking became extremely rigid (the great danger of type (1) planning), which led to disaster in Vietnam. But this was due to the misuse and abuse of policy, not its existence.

The Cold War consensus existed because the global situation looked to Americans like a straightforward struggle between good and evil. In the absence of such a vision, consensus can be hard to maintain—but not impossible. For better or worse, the gap between many countries' political parties on foreign policy issues is narrow. No major European party advocated the abandonment of NATO during the Cold War. None of the political parties in the Western democracies felt favorably toward Hitler. In Germany before World War II, the foreign policy debates were sharper, but even many non-Nazis were angry about Poland's growth at the expense of Germany.[20] Precisely because the world is now so unstable and unsettled, rigid type (1) planning is an academic exercise. For the same reason, few political parties have very specific foreign policy positions. This is therefore an excellent period to rethink policy. Specific plans are not needed, and the absence of an immediate crisis provides a bit of breathing space.

The second way to get around the inherent problems of type (1) planning is to focus on the one type of planning we have not really talked about yet—type (2), how decisions will be made. This is the most important and the most difficult of the three types of decision-making. Its importance lies in the environment in which decisions are made. Because crises and wars have a momentum of their own, many decisions have to be made that could not be prepared in advance, or even foreseen. The longer or more serious the crisis or war, the more important the quality of decision-making becomes.

The difficulty of type (2) planning has to do with who may participate.

---

20. As a result they supported Hitler's foreign policy, which resulted in even more of Germany becoming Polish.

If you try to decide how decisions are to be made, you quickly realize that it is not just a function of who makes the final decision, or how intelligent that final decision-maker is. Rather, it is a function of who will have input in the decision. Too few participants, and the result is too little information or diversity of thought; too many, and the outcome will be confusion or even chaos. How will information be gathered, distributed, interpreted? What kind of a command structure is in place? Does the national leader directly command every military unit? It would certainly simplify the chain of command, but chaos on the battlefield would be all but inevitable. Some things have to be delegated, but deciding which things is controversial.

When we look at how these problems have been addressed in the real world, we see that no country has ever found a perfect solution (there probably isn't one), and that there are as many different ways of doing it as there are governments. Take dictatorships. It is not clear whether dictatorships command more efficiently than democracies in crises and wars, because dictatorships have not all acted alike. During World War II, two dictatorships—Hitler's Germany and Stalin's Soviet Union—fought the bitterest war in history. Each man was as fully in control of his country as was humanly possible. But important differences existed in how decisions were made. In Germany, the command structure was inefficient and divided, united only by Hitler's personal military staff. In Soviet Russia, the war effort was well centralized at the military and civilian levels; while Stalin kept an extremely close eye on these bodies (and this meant something!), they were not just extensions of his personal dictatorship. In Germany, Hitler increasingly issued commands without consulting his generals about what was possible. Stalin was much more inclined to listen and allow the generals to develop proposals, although there never was any question but that even technical details had to be submitted to him for approval (no one ever had to be reminded of this twice).

The experience and behavior of the dictatorships are is surprisingly relevant. Even democratic governments behave in quite authoritarian ways during crisis and war. Virtually every American war president has behaved dictatorially in some ways. Indeed, the Constitution allows this, although obviously not on a level comparable with Hitler or Stalin. Military institutions gain great autonomy in war, somctimes running the war effort without interference. The results of this autonomy are mixed. To take a well-known European example, in 1914 Germany was a monarchy with democratic institutions, which allowed its army to make the crucial decisions that year, and then permitted the army's commanders to run the war effort more or less without oversight. The military had a free hand, yet it lost (to be fair, it was fighting armies that also had great, if less, freedom).

The American experience with type (2) planning is as complicated as any to be found in history because the paths of decision are sometimes unclear, despite the Constitution's deceptively simple language on the subject. Article I gives Congress the power to establish the military and the regulations that govern it, and to declare war; the Second Amendment ensures that states may continue to arm themselves (although Washington can take over state forces); and Article II provides that the president of the United States can recognize foreign goverments (giving him control of much of foreign policy) and, most important, that he "shall be Commander in Chief" of the armed forces.

That seems wonderfully clear and simple, but this last phrase has caused much mischief. The meaning of "commander in chief" is not defined. It could mean that the president can take the field with the army. Alternatively, it could be interpreted to mean that the president can do with the military whatever he wishes, including sending it to Bosnia, bombing Iraq, or blowing up the planet. Or the constitutional truth may lie somewhere in between. The answer has changed over time. The Constitution came into effect during the tenure of a president who had taken the field with the army. His successor fought this country's first undeclared war (1798–1799), indicating that even 200 years ago the Constitution was somewhat elastic.

This elasticity was proven by the enormous power accumulated by Abraham Lincoln during the Civil War. Lincoln used the "commander in chief" clause to abolish slavery in the rebellious territories, imprison people without trial, and conduct the war more or less as he wished, although a joint congressional committee did attempt to oversee the war effort. Even so, the war powers of the presidency then were less than they are now.

Presidential power has blossomed this century, and the president's power to act militarily has grown as well. This was a function of America's growth into a global empire, the advent of military technology that required quick decisions, and the expansion of a national security bureaucracy that is under the president's direct command. The passage of the War Powers Act (1975) attempted to set some outside limits on presidential powers, but this law has never been tested in court. So we can assume that the president will continue to have enormous power over military and foreign affairs and therefore will remain at the center of decision-making.

In reality, however, the president's crisis and war powers are not as great as they seem. There are so many groups and institutions that can pressure the White House to change course that it is impossible to enumerate them all; I will consider only the obvious ones. Congress as a whole controls the purse strings. The Senate has an ill-defined "advice and consent" power regarding foreign policy, and it has to ratify all treaties (which means the president cannot guarantee that a crisis resolution will be accepted back home, and this is an enormous limitation indeed on his power). Public opinion plays a much greater role in foreign policy than is generally realized; with the introduction of talk radio and other electronic communications means, as well as sophisticated polling, public opinion is more visible than ever. National security bureaucracies (the Pentagon, the individual services, the CIA, the NSA, the State Department, etc.) each have their own agendas. Their advice to the president is neither neutral nor disinterested. Multinational corporations and banks will have their say, and only a foolish president would ignore them. Other non-governmental organizations, such as unions, clerical, humanitarian and charitable associations, and emigre or ethnic groups can be quite influential. In 1945, Polish Americans were a formidable bloc of voters, demanding a hard line against Soviet occupation of Poland. Since 1948, American Jews have been strongly sympathetic to Israel. American Blacks encouraged the U.S. government to oppose the apartheid policies of South Africa. Today, the Cuban exile community in Florida vigorously insists that the government maintain its economic stranglehold on Fidel Castro's Cuba.

These complex weaknesses in presidential power have been understood by all successful war presidents (and misunderstood by the failures). Abraham Lincoln won the Civil War partly because he solved some of these problems. He created an independent military chain of command (while Jefferson Davis tried to run the war by himself). Lincoln also built Yankee unity around the twin issues of national reunification and abolition of slavery. Finally, he waited and allowed the South to make the fatal error of firing the first shot. The Lincoln-Davis contrast is particularly instructive, as the same point in time produced two American war presidents dealing with similar cultural and political problems. Davis was a soldier who had become secretary of war and knew much more about military problems than did Lincoln. He also had the luxury of participating in the writing of his own constitution (which mirrored the U.S.

version in most ways). Davis was unsuccessful in virtually everything he did, but his biggest shortcoming was his inability to unify his country. Lincoln coped far better with the lack of unity, somehow working in a political spectrum that ranged from Southern sympathizers to the Radical Republicans. Davis failed even to make peace with his vice president. Lincoln attempted to centralize military command early, while Davis did not appoint a military commander in chief until 1865. Instead, he intervened personally on several occasions, notably during the Union attacks on Vicksburg and Atlanta. His intervention led to two of the Confederacy's worst defeats.

Perhaps feeling that Lincoln was a better role model than Davis, Franklin D. Roosevelt unified military control under himself, bypassing Cabinet departments, about two months before World War II officially began. Harry Truman established his position as commander in chief by firing the popular General Douglas MacArthur, who had forgotten where he stood in the chain of command. Note that all three of these successful war presidents appreciated that decisions could only be successful if they were effective—that is, if they were actually carried out.

The above sounds as if centralization solves all problems. Obviously, a completely decentralized system could not survive for long. Many of its resources would be wasted and used for contradictory purposes. Centralization does not solve all problems, however, for two reasons. First, too much centralization can stifle creativity. An army, for example, may have to act as one, but if it thinks as one, it becomes inflexible and loses its ability to adapt to changing circumstances. Second, too much centralization gives the leader too much to do in terms of details, and the results can be unfortunate (except for the enemy). Hitler's centralization contributed mightily to Nazi Germany's defeat. Stalin's centralization nearly did the same in 1941, because the system's dependence on his decisions led to paralysis. In addition, the dictator's refusal to believe that Hitler would attack him caused subordinates to stop giving him intelligence information predicting such an attack. Countless millions died because of the failures of these two heavily centralized dictatorships.

Another proposed "magic bullet" is to leave the conduct of war and crisis management to experts, whether diplomats during a crisis or soldiers in wartime. There are only two problems with this idea: It won't work in the United States, and it hasn't always worked elsewhere. It won't work here because it would require the president to delegate his powers to others to an extent that might be illegal and, more significant, would not be tolerated.

During the Vietnam War many critics thought that there was too little delegation, arguing that the soldiers were fighting the war "with one hand tied behind their backs." The war effort might not have been significantly better, however, if the military had conducted it with less interference. The reason that it would not is quite simple: The generals were never in agreement about how the war ought to be fought. There never was a clear "military versus civilian" conception of the war. In any event, leaving crises and wars to experts would be unworkable given the many groups with influence on foreign policy, and it ignores one rather obvious fact: Armies fight battles, but nations wage wars. It would be remarkable if this entire nation would place its destiny over a long period of time in the hands of a small group of experts.

The idea of leaving crises and wars in the hands of experts has had its share of failures elsewhere in modern times. In World War I, governments would have benefited from ignoring or overruling military leadership once in a while; the most extreme case occurred in 1917 when German submarines nearly destroyed Britain by sinking huge numbers of merchant vessels. The Royal Navy adamantly opposed the use of the convoy system (grouping ships together under warship escort) and wanted merchants to continue to sail individually. The Royal Navy believed that convoys would make bigger targets and raise losses. The government in fact did step in and overrule the "experts," and Britain survived.

This does not prove, or even suggest, that civilian leaders should ignore or overrule soldiers whenever the urge strikes. There are too many examples of leaders losing wars because of excessive interference; Jefferson Davis and Hitler (both former soldiers, ironically) come to mind. Successful war leaders do give their soldiers great leeway without giving them total freedom, and, more important, are familiar enough with the history and concepts of war to be strategists in their own right, to know when to overrule their soldiers and when to leave them alone. We have established in the United States that there are no magic formulas or slogans that guarantee that the decision-making process, which is what type (2) is all about, will be successful.

That does not mean that guidelines cannot be laid down. In Chapter 7, I will suggest specific recommendations for the future, which will include suggestions on how to improve our decision-making process. To the government's credit, the system has been improved since the Vietnam fiasco, but serious problems remain. Rivalries among the military services, and between and with various civilian agencies, continue.

Without a Cold War, there is no longer a bipartisan foreign policy consensus, and with every other year being an election year, public pressure is more important and more volatile than ever. Ideologues and fanatics are always trying to make the global facts fit their prejudices. This was exemplified by Hitler, perhaps explaining why he was defeated by the more objective and realistic Stalin. So far, Americans have resisted the temptation to elect anyone from the radical extremes to the presidency. But in a crisis, this could change. Global instability now is greater than at any time since the 1920s. A leadership that thinks about possible future crises, learns from the past and knows the importance of remaining calm and flexible in a crisis can survive this era. Only if the whole decision-making process is organized with these goals in mind is it likely that the leadership will behave with the intelligence and judgment needed for survival. This is particularly important in regard to a leadership's ability to assess objectively and compensate for the nation's weaknesses, which we will now consider.

6

CHINKS IN THE ARMOR

The United States has almost become used to being a great power. I say almost, because fifty-five years after America's entry into World War II, there is plenty of evidence that Americans are not totally comfortable with the idea. No country has sent more troops to more places around the globe than America, and yet no country debates troop deployment with such vigor. Even the sending of contingents to Haiti became an issue, despite the fact that the United States has sent soldiers to the Caribbean basin with gay abandon for almost a century. No country has had more influence on structuring the modern world than the United States, yet few countries' peoples are more suspicious of that same world. The United Nations, the World Bank (IBRD), the International Monetary Fund, the Council on Foreign Relations, the Trilateral Commission—all grist for the mill of American conspiracy theorists, yet all were established with heavy American influence.

Americans are not used to superpower status because it came relatively recently, and because we were not used to thinking about international politics at all. Countries with powerful neighbors get used to the complex ins and outs of international relations, but Americans still look for simple answers, clear and straightforward solutions, and interventions with artificial time limits. These attitudes come from geography and history, not ignorance. The United States was virtually invulnerable until the advent of planes and missiles with intercontinental capabilities. The

British might burn coastal cities during the War of 1812, but they could never have reconquered the whole country. It was just too big. The only American acquisitions close to substantial foreign powers were Alaska (purchased from Russia in 1867) and the Philippines (seized from Spain in 1898), obtained only after vigorous domestic debate. The Philippines would become the American empire's Achilles heel in the 1930s, but in 1898 none of East Asia's major states were a potential threat. China was rent by internal division and threatened by increasing pressure from Russia and Japan, neither of which had powerful enough naval forces to threaten the Philippines. Japan had only begun to acquire a modern navy, while the hollowness of Russia's strength (and, indeed, of Russia itself) became apparent in the Russo-Japanese War (1904–1905). Alaska was even less vulnerable. It might be close to Russia, but the climate and terrain that far north rendered conventional military attacks virtually impossible.

The Japanese attack on Pearl Harbor in 1941 came as a great shock to this sense of security, but Pearl was far from the American heartland. Axis contact with the American mainland remained minimal throughout World War II. A few German spies and sailors set foot on American shores, and a few people were killed when Japanese balloons, loaded with explosives, floated across the Pacific, but that was it; only Hawaii and Alaska briefly saw significant action. Only after the war, and especially with the introduction of rockets and the Soviet launch of the Sputnik satellite (1957) did the geographical invulnerability start to disappear. The greatest loss of security did not come from Soviet rockets, but from America's need for imported natural resources. This was, however, a more subtle shift in our international position that did not immediately penetrate the public mind.

The public mind of America had been formed—as is always the case —by the national historical experience. In terms of global contacts, this experience goes back to the beginning of the country. The American revolutionaries were heavily involved in international affairs. In one way or another, France, Spain, and Holland were on the American side, and the inflow of foreign aid was substantial. Otherwise, Britain might have won the Revolutionary War. Yet this did not translate into any American desire to get involved in European affairs. Why not? The American involvement with foreign powers had been largely to secure independence, nothing more. Many Americans saw the "old world" of Europe as corrupt, and believed that the less association with its great powers, the better. The two political parties of that day were more or less united on this point (which makes it all the more interesting that the two parties of our day were united in favor of the opposite, Cold War interventionism).

This did not mean that the early republic was unwilling to fight to protect its short-term interests. By 1815, America had fought wars against both France and Britain, and twice sent warships to protect American commerce in the Mediterranean. But the new United States made no global long-term alliances and formulated no global long-term policies because, in a sense, it had no global long-term interests. It merely wished to keep foreign powers out of its own neighborhood, and as no foreign power really wished to push the issue, American foreign policy in the nineteenth century remains a remarkably dull subject. American warships did engage in some gunboat diplomacy at the expense of Japan in 1853–1854, but the latter was hardly a significant power then. France and Britain did attempt to develop a closer relationship with the Republic of Texas (1836–1845), but this merely sped up the annexation of Texas. It is a measure of historical U.S. concern about borderland threats that the annexation occurred despite the deep domestic problems it would cause. Texas' successful war for independence in 1836 had not been followed by annexation because Texas' admission would disrupt the slave state-free state balance. In 1844–1845, however, this concern was eclipsed by the growing rapprochement between Texas and two of the old European colonial powers. The outcome of this annexation also led to the conquest of the entire Southwest at Mexico's expense, completing most of the Manifest Destiny vision but creating some constitutional and cultural problems as well.

The only other significant intervention in the neighborhood occurred when France decided to create a Mexican throne for an Austrian prince while America was occupied by the Civil War. This project began as a three power debt-collection exercise in 1862, but France's Napoleon III's ambition to turn Mexico into a monarchy headed by the unfortunate Maximilian caused the others to pull out. The United States was not happy about this event but at that moment could do nothing. The Civil War prevented a response in three ways. Military intervention was out, as the Union needed all its soldiers to defeat the rebellion. Diplomatic intervention was impossible because of the need to keep France from recognizing the Confederacy. Finally, Texas was a Confederate state, and until the Confederacy was suppressed, hardly a safe base for Union military threats against Maximilian. At the end of the Civil War, however, things changed. President Andrew Johnson sent 100,000 troops to the Rio Grande and, although overt threats were lacking, the hint was enough. The French army left Mexico, and the government of the beleaguered Maximilian collapsed. Three years later, the same thing happened to Napoleon III.

These European efforts at intervention in the Western Hemisphere were feeble and in no way a threat to the United States (neither were they intended to be). If anything, America's position improved. Canada ceased to be a true "colony" of Britain shortly after the Civil War, gaining internal self-government. With the purchase of Alaska, the United States faced less major-power presence in the Western Hemisphere than it had at the beginning of the century.

As the nineteenth century wore on, the United States entered a period of explosive growth. The national economy became the world's largest, the West was conquered and settled, and the population doubled. By the end of the century, the United States had everything—wealth, land and people—that is traditionally necessary to become a great power. What it lacked was a good reason for becoming one. All this changed in 1898, when the Spanish-American War led the United States to add Guam, Puerto Rico, Cuba, and the Philippines—in one stroke becoming a Pacific/Asian/Caribbean power. Bitter arguments ensued between those who, like Theodore Roosevelt, felt that America would become a great power and should do it on its own terms, and those who felt that foreign holdings were contrary to American traditions.

In a way, both sides of that argument won. America kept the new territories but remained detached from the tensions and clashes between the other major powers. American forces did travel to Central America and the Caribbean whenever American interests dictated it. American soldiers did go to China to help other powers suppress a rebellion but did so to protect American interests there, not to start a long-term relationship with foreign powers. The U.S. Army had to wage a bitter and controversial war in the Philippines to hang on to that archipelago, but that was after the decision to annex had become law. The United States lived in the best of all possible worlds; it could intervene in small or medium-size crises when it wished to, but nothing could jeopardize its existence or security.

This situation continued until 1917 when the United States entered World War I and became, in every sense of the word, a great power. By war's end, the United States had sent 2 million soldiers to fight in Europe, joined an international military alliance, and dominated international diplomacy. Here, however, the old uncertainty about being a great power reared its head. President Woodrow Wilson hoped to keep peace by creating a League of Nations, an ancestor of the United Nations. It was created, but we were not in it. The League treaty went down to defeat in the U.S. Senate because too many people thought that it was inherently a bad idea or that it would infringe on American independence (Wilson's principled ineptitude also affected the outcome of the vote). This decision for non-involvement had far-reaching consequences. Without the United States, the League was too weak to have much effect on the designs of the Nazis, fascists, and militarists who led the planet into global war and the Holocaust. The United States also played no role in the efforts of some European nations to hem Hitler in. When World War II broke out in 1939, the United States was still relatively isolated.

Three things combined to change the American position from a strong but isolated country to one with a military and diplomatic presence everywhere. First, President Franklin D. Roosevelt began to prepare the country for war and edged toward confrontation with Nazi Germany and militarist Japan. The United States put pressure on Japan to cease its aggression against China and started to help Britain in its death struggle against Nazi Germany. Second, the Japanese attack on Pearl Harbor led the United States into a direct military confrontation with the Axis powers (Japan, Germany, and Italy). By the time it was over, the United States had military forces spread around the globe, many other powers were dependent on the United States for economic help, and the historical relationship between America and Europe had been completely reversed. America was No. 1.

The third reason for becoming a great power was, of course, the Cold War. Unlike after World War I, America did not revert to isolationism again.[21] Whatever the public ambivalence about great-power status had been, it was swept away by waves of fear of Soviet Russia and communism, which were seen as direct threats to America. In other words, the old battle about isolationism versus interventionism was not settled because people's support for the Cold War was based on the idea that America itself was being attacked. Such a perception would have produced a response a hundred years ago as well.

On the other hand, the way in which the United States chose the wage to Cold War was quite different from the past. The idea of pulling back to California and New York and leaving the rest of the world to its own

---

21. To be fair, a number of scholars have argued that the United States was not truly "isolated" after World War I.

problems was dead (or so it seemed). World War II had killed it. If Pearl Harbor accomplished anything, it was to convince Americans (for a while, anyway) that their fate was not separate from events overseas. Instead of withdrawing, the United States:

- founded an international organization (the United Nations).
- established international financial organizations (the World Bank (IBRD) and the International Monetary Fund).
- organized and funded the most powerful military establishment in history.
- created an alphabet soup of national security and espionage agencies.
- created and joined foreign military alliances, most notably the North Atlantic Treaty Organization (NATO).

Contrast this with America's past practices, including

- voting down an international organization (the League of Nations).
- dissolving its own central national bank.
- maintaining an army of only 25,000 men in the later nineteenth century.
- organizing no new major defense-related agencies in the previous century and a half.
- avoiding (on George Washington's advice) all "entangling alliances."

Not only had the United States become a great power, it had created a new category: Superpower. For half a century, the United States contested for global power, opposing the Soviet Union and its allies while fighting (or claiming to fight) an ideological force called communism, although many moderate leftist groups were swept into this category as well. The American public and its two political parties solidly supported the Cold War. There was surprisingly little public disagreement over foreign policy until the Vietnam War, and even thereafter the disputes were more over means than ends. For a half century there was strong support for large military budgets, an interventionist policy, and substantial foreign aid (as long as it was linked to Cold War strategy). To be sure, the United States was hardly the same country at the end of the Cold War that it had been at the beginning. The Cold War was not a seamless whole. In 1969, for example, President Richard Nixon and his adviser, Henry Kissinger (later secretary of state), recognized that America's relative military and economic power was slipping and that a more accommodating policy (detente) toward the Soviet Union was necessary. Fortunately (for us) the Soviet Union was also experiencing problems, which helps explain the Nixon-Kissinger success in readjusting Cold War strategy. The changes they wrought, however, did not affect the long-term public and bipartisan support for Cold War policy (although it was certainly at a low point when they entered office).

Nixon and Kissinger appeared on the scene when the United States was at an exceptionally dangerous point. Economic stagnation, not yet fully recognized, was beginning, as was a pattern of inflation. Nixon was seriously concerned about the economic effects of the winding down of the Vietnam War effort. The domestic scene was one of unparalleled protests and riots, extremist dissent on the left and right, and three-way political warfare among the government, the civil rights movement, and the Southern establishment over integration. The relationship with NATO was strained because of Vietnam, and several NATO countries were experiencing turmoil (especially, inevitably, France). The Soviet Union was reaching nuclear parity with the United States at the very moment that America's conventional forces had deteriorated in quality. Equipment was aging because much of the defense budget had to pay the day-to-day costs of the war. More important, the atmosphere in and outside the military had been poisoned by the Vietnam experience. In other words, when Nixon became president, the country's four most potent sources of strength—political unity, economic stability, nuclear superiority, and conventional military strength—were all eroding. To a casual observer, it might have appeared that an era of Soviet Cold War dominance was about to begin.

This was not what happened. The Soviet Union's internal problems were far worse than America's. In addition, Nixon slowly pulled the United States out of Vietnam, deftly stifled domestic dissent, and pursued detente with the Soviet Union. The withdrawal relied on occasional local escalations as well, designed to prove that the will and ability to use force were intact. Kissinger's efforts to link detente and Vietnam proved unavailing, however. Campus dissent declined markedly after the draft board system was abolished, however, and— perhaps more significant—the draft calls declined. The Southern establishment was placated by the administration's anti-busing policy. The civil rights movement was partly coopted through a variety of Nixon administration initiatives that, even if they appeared insincere (and probably were), at least had a calming effect. Detente, of course, was the most visible part of the Nixon-Kissinger strategy, but it ultimately succeeded only because of the Soviet Union's domestic troubles and Nixon's willingness to make threats at critical moments to disabuse the Soviet leadership of the idea that America had become a Maoist paper tiger. The main result of Nixon's policies was that the United States emerged from this critical midpoint in the Cold War sufficiently intact in a strategic sense to survive even a president like Jimmy Carter, and able to hope for a positive resolution of the Cold War. In fact, the country got more than it bargained for.

The end of the Cold War was dramatic. The leader of the Soviet Union began to dismantle the whole ramshackle communist edifice whose existence had provided the (American) justification for the Cold War, and he then began drastically to reduce the Soviet military presence in Eastern Europe (which had helped trigger the Cold War). The American president, a veteran Cold Warrior, responded diplomatically, and the U.S.-Soviet relationship reached unimaginably warm levels. Then, the entire Soviet Union collapsed. At the risk of belaboring the obvious, it was not Soviet leader Mikhail Gorbachev's intent to dissolve his country. Gorbachev hoped to save communism by modernizing it. The removal of the Soviet military presence in Eastern Europe was designed to assure Western nations—especially Germany—of Soviet intentions and to secure foreign investment, while reducing the immense Soviet defense expenditures. Gorbachev did not see the survival of the Soviet system in terms of having an island of communist nations headed by himself. He cheerfully pulled the plug on many Soviet clients, including Cuba and Nicaragua, and began moving out of the Horn of Africa and Angola as well. In a sense, the Cold War ended because Gorbachev had become an evolutionary socialist, rather than a traditional communist viewing everything in terms of class and global struggle. This explains his domestic program as well. The removal of restrictions on freedom of expression *(glasnost')* was intended to produce bottom-up restructuring *(perestroika)* and, in a sense, it did; but Gorbachev perhaps overestimated the system's ability to control the process. So did the United States, by the way. As a result, the collapse, which surprised most (but not, contrary to popular opinion, all) observers, created a peculiar situation. While the United States was the survivor of the Cold War and, therefore, the victor, the victory was marred by some major problems.

First, the United States neither sought nor desired the Soviet collapse at the time it came. President George Bush even flew to the Ukraine to publicly beg its nationalist leaders not to dissolve the Soviet Union. Not surprisingly, his visit was ineffectual. By 1991, the U.S. government feared post-Soviet instability more than the Soviet Union, and with good reason. The instability caused by the decline or collapse of a great power creates a greater risk of war than a confrontation like the Cold War. Both world wars can be traced to problems that followed great-power collapses. The World War I had its roots in the collapse of the Ottoman Empire (Turkey) in Europe, which began a century earlier but happened mainly after 1878. This created a zone of instability in which new countries were formed. In this zone, empires such as Austria and Russia had competing interests that helped eventually lead them to war in 1914. World War II was certainly sped along by the collapse of the Austrian Empire and the temporary decline of the Russian Empire. The former disappeared, the latter lost its western territories and was isolated from most of the world. A new group of states arose on the wreckage, an unstable situation exploited cleverly and ruthlessly by Adolf Hitler. Chaos followed collapse and created the environment for total war.

Second, the American people did not receive the benefits that they had expected to accrue at the end of the Cold War. The assumption was that a victory in the Cold War would solve the world's problems, allow for huge budget and tax cuts, and allow the United States to do something besides being a "global policeman." None of those three things happened. Many of the world's problems are more severe now than during the Cold War. Defense spending has leveled off, but has not declined enough to make much of a difference to the average taxpayer. The U.S. military establishment is smaller than it used to be, but we still field the world's most powerful military. Finally, the role of the United States has not so much changed as it has become unclear.

There is some argument about why this is so. One popular suggestion is that the United States' foreign policy woes result from the lack of an enemy. For fifty years, the United States had a clear enemy (or thought so) and now, all of a sudden, that enemy is gone. The evidence for this argument seems strong. We do seem to scan for a new threat, be it Iran, the Medellin and Cali cartels, or whatever. The Soviet foreign minister in that country's closing years even claimed that it was his policy to deprive America of an enemy. His view was somewhat ahistorical, however. It was the Russian/Soviet state, not America, that developed in an atmosphere of a "permanent threat." The Russian state evolved in response to hostile threats from Mongols, Lithuanians, Swedes, Poles, and Turks. Not surprisingly, the Russian people found the Marxist-Leninist view of the inevitability of struggle as a highly natural description of the order of things. That was not the case here, of course. American culture and foreign policy could easily function without a threat, except that this would require an impossible reversion to an isolated world as well. The only loss from the American popular perspective is that the familiarity of the Cold War bipolar struggle has disappeared. Enemy scanning does occur; it happens, however, because of America's position in the world, and that leads directly to the core of the problem.

The real cause of today's uncertainty is America's failure to come completely to terms with its great-power status. Just as the Cold War enjoyed bipartisan support, isolationism also receives support from a surprisingly broad array of people, speaking from many different ideologies. The American Right's thinking is exemplified by Jesse Helms, in particular his view of foreign aid as inherently wasteful, and by Patrick Buchanan, who sees the global economy as a plaything for the rich. This latter view is shared on the Left by labor unions, which see trade as a threat to jobs, while more traditional leftists like Noam Chomsky see American foreign involvement as having been largely a force for evil. Chomsky and Helms are so far apart that we have to ask ourselves how these spokesmen of the radical extremes can reflect with similar negativity about American interaction with the rest of the planet. In essence, both the Left and the Right see the world system as corrupt. The Left sees the world system as an extension of capitalist excess. The Right suspects that the world system is the harbinger of socialism.

These tendencies toward isolationism reflect a heartfelt American attitude: namely, that the country should get involved abroad only if its vital interests or national security are at stake, and that otherwise, we should stay out. As I have suggested above, this stems from the unique history and geography enjoyed by America. In addition, Americans expect their foreign involvements to be crusades; Americans see themselves as knights sallying forth from Europe to save the Holy Land, or, perhaps, as the cavalry arriving to save helpless settlers. If the reality of the situation conflicts with this hope, the gut reaction is straightforward: withdraw.

There would be nothing at all wrong with this, provided that it reflected a consistent national view toward the world. It does not. Rather, we have a reversion to the historical attitude of isolationism when it suits us, but support for intervention when we have to; in other words, an episodic interventionism. This would work over the long haul only if America could dictate the pace of world events. The trouble with this is that America can dictate the pace of world events only if she is constantly involved in those events; in other words, in order not to be the world's policeman, the United States has to police the world.

None of this by itself does much harm to the argument of the consistent isolationist, and in Chapter 7 I will incorporate some aspects of isolationism in my proposals. An isolationist position would require, however, that America accept certain limitations on its activities abroad —that is, after all, the definition of isolationism.

There are three such limitations. First, America would have to stop importing raw materials. This is our greatest source of vulnerability. Second, America would have to admit that it cannot and will not protect its citizens abroad. Finally, America would have to be willing to let world events, including potential threats, ebb and flow without responding until the results landed on our shores.

Some aspects of isolationism would have little appeal to the nation, and it is useless to propose strategies that have no chance of passing political muster. The only way to reduce oil imports, for example, would be through stringent conservation, exploitation of alternative energy sources and much higher fuel prices (which would raise the price of everything else). Isolationism would cost lots of money. Inflation and unemployment would soar. We would actually be more secure, but would the nation accept the price? Not taking action against countries or terrorists harming Americans abroad would hardly be popular. Sanctions against Iran and Cuba, for example, would logically have to end. Parts of this isolationist program might be acceptable, but the whole package would not.

Given the difficulty of turning isolationist theory into practice, it is no surprise that American isolationism has had decidedly mixed results. Thomas Jefferson imposed a trade embargo on Britain and France, rather than risk war with either, during his last two years in office, and he opted for a coast defense strategy rather than an expensive navy. The failure of Jefferson's policies led his successor into the War of 1812, such a total fiasco that Jefferson's isolationist foreign policy looks a little better—but only a little. His use of sanctions, rather than force, resonated throughout American history. Jefferson Davis employed sanctions to force Britain into recognizing the Confederacy; like Jefferson, Davis failed. The list of unsuccessful sanctions is too long to compress even into an entire chapter. The only time that sanctions worked was during World War II, when the United States imposed economic sanctions on Japan because it was angry about Japan's invasion of China, and wanted Japan to change its policy. (Franklin D. Roosevelt could not do anything more because isolationist sentiment was if anything stronger then than it had been before.) His sanctions were a success in that they did cause Japan to change its policy, although not in the way that was hoped. Roosevelt and most Americans hoped for a Japanese withdrawal from China. Instead, Japan attacked the United States, damaging the U.S. Pacific Fleet and devastating the isolationists.

Or so it was thought. The rhetoric of World War II and the Cold War convinced many that American isolationism was dead, but it is not. For the "average American," isolationism holds considerable appeal. This seems odd, since the historical record of American isolationism is at best mixed. Part of the answer is geography. The other part of the answer is more complicated and lies in the country's self-image, and is in fact one of the greatest "chinks in the armor" that Americans have to consider as they face their future, and that of their country. As stated earlier, Americans have never come to terms with their country's being a great power.

Roughly speaking, America has gone through four stages, and is now entering a fifth. During the first (1607–1775) America was only an extension of another great power, Britain. The colonists were not passive players, of course. They participated actively in efforts to drive the French out of North America (although this turned out to be a Pyrrhic victory[22]). Colonial leaders actively encouraged the British government to take various actions (mostly hostile) against Spain and France, and began the eighteenth century's biggest war (French and Indian/Seven Years' War). The colonists did not constitute a sovereign power, of course, but they did have definite foreign policy views by the time the Revolution began in 1775.

From 1775 to about 1890, America was firmly isolationist, viewing Europe's great-power politics as corrupt and unimportant. Between 1890 and 1945, the United States advanced toward great power status, but amid much debate and dissension. To be sure, there were genuinely imperialist views inside America, some business-related, some more

---

22. Colonial merchants lost money as their illegal French trade dried up, while the British were saddled with war debts for which they tried to tax the colonies and their trade. The result was a bigger disaster for the British—the American Revolution.

principled (such as those of Alfred Thayer Mahan and Theodore Roosevelt), but those views could hardly have prevailed without German and Japanese aggression. From 1945 until 1991, the United States was consumed by the Cold War, during which advocacy of isolationism was visible only on the ideological peripheries of the extreme right and left, which, for different reasons, saw (and see) all world events as the results of conspiracies anyway. So, while America has been a great power for at least a quarter of its history, and some would say closer to half, many Americans are uncomfortable with this fact (while still willing to accept the benefits of great-power status) and mistrust the whole idea.

This mistrust is rooted in the nature of great-power status. Great powers must rely on *realpolitik,* a pragmatic approach to international politics. America has done so, but its people are not comfortable with the lack of moral basis implied by such a policy. Great-power foreign policy is (and has to be) made by small elites in the capital city, which runs counter to the (healthy) American mistrust of healthy elites and the capital city. Great-power politics requires the making (and breaking) of alliances, but alliances also are not popular in America (or many other countries) because they can limit freedom of action. Finally, successful foreign policy requires consistency over time, which is always difficult in the United States and is about to get more difficult: Our foreign policy is highly politicized.

During the Cold War, partisan rhetoric, in a sense, did not matter because the two political parties were fairly close together on how to deal with communism, the Soviet Union, and so on. With the end of the Cold War, political debates over foreign policy became more important and more dangerous. "Sound bite" politics might be bad for domestic affairs, but they are disastrous for foreign policy. Government exercises much more control over foreign than domestic affairs; bad domestic policy might never have any effect, while bad foreign policy can cause World War III. In addition, the audience (voters) is probably a bit better informed about what's happening at home than about abroad. One of our most notorious chinks in the armor is that people are generally ignorant concerning foreign affairs.

The size, military power, and geographical safety of the United States have added up to a situation in which the average American has not needed to know much about foreign countries. The United States has fought four major foreign wars this century, however, and the impact of events abroad on America will grow, not shrink. Paradoxically, isolationism could work only if the country was exceptionally well informed about world events. Educators are trying to remedy this situation somewhat by stressing "globalization" or "internationalization" of school curricula, but this will probably have little effect. Global ignorance does not come from a lack of information—there is plenty of information available—but from the attitude described above. As a result, world events and trends appear on the American screen only when a real crisis occurs, preferably one directly involving American troops, and then the result is confusion, not education, in the public mind. Inevitably this produces in some the paranoid tendency of "enemy scanning," which is based on the assumptions that the whole world is divided into pro- and anti-American forces and that our entire foreign policy should consist of finding and fighting the enemies. There is a certain logic to this tendency because America's history as a great power is almost entirely linked to a series of wars; therefore, what makes more sense than to view great power politics as a form of warfare, preferably warfare involving some great moral issue?

Our world view is dominated by enemy scanning. One of the more interesting forms of enemy scanning—repeated by some European figures as well as Americans—is the idea that a conflict is pending between "the West" and "Islam." This perceived threat has been called "the specter of Islam" (Muslims, by the way, do not believe in specters). While some Islamic states can and do view the United States as an enemy (Iran and the Sudan come to mind), the idea that an entire religion is going to unite against a state or group of states is simply ahistorical. To put it another way, it has never happened. Muslims know this, and know quite well that Islam has not been united since the seventh century. Christians might search for a period when their religion united them all against a common enemy, and they would search in vain. But there are other fallacies. Islam, by itself, is a religion, not a political force. The West is also not monolithic, and does not present a clear unitary alternative to Islam. Islamists (fanatical, politically minded Muslims) are most likely to oppose secularism, not Christianity. On the other hand, Europe is more secular and less religious than America, which is home to several million Muslims, yet Islamists seem to have more of a quarrel with America than with Europe. The fanatics in the Muslim world appear far more interested in expelling "Western" influences than in exporting their own views. Finally, Islam is neither a Middle Eastern nor an Arab religion primarily, but is centered today in the East, with its largest following in Indonesia. Fanatical movements in the Muslim world could certainly be regarded as a threat—and should be—but the same is true of such movements inside Western countries as well.

The history of warfare between different cultural and religious groups does not provide much evidence that the battle of the Mediterranean is about to break out. Most of these conflicts have been over territory and economic factors. The wars between the Christian West and the Muslim rulers were mostly traditional conflicts in which religion was used as a powerful motivator, but was not the cause. In the eighth century, a Muslim people known as the Moors overran Spain; between 1085 and 1492, the Spaniards and the Portuguese overthrew and expelled them. Militant Catholicism was a powerful weapon in these Crusade-like wars, but the desire to get rid of an essentially foreign set of rulers was probably an even greater force. The Crusades themselves (beginning in 1096) did have a much more religious character, but the behavior of Europe's Christian nobles in the Holy Land suggests that many had non-religious motives for going. In the later Crusades, their biggest impact was the undermining of Christian Constantinople. Finally, the truly Christian among these combatants had the Holy Land as a goal, a very specific theo-military target that in no way included an endless war for the destruction of a competing religion or culture. (In fact, the most significant threat to Islamic culture as a whole came not from Christian Europe, but from the Mongol-Ilkhanid state in the 13th century.) The wars between the Ottoman Empire and various Christian states were predominantly over territory. When the Turks stormed Constantinople (1453), only minimal assistance arrived from the rest of Christian Europe. In the seventeenth century foreign armies did move to relieve Vienna from the Turkish threat (1683) but this was simple self-preservation; Vienna lies in the heart of Europe. By the same token, the Turks did not invade Christian Europe for purely religious reasons; they were just as willing to conquer Islamic peoples, such as the Arabs. In 1854, European armies did participate in a Middle Eastern war, but that was to help Islamic Turkey against another Christian state, Russia.

In 1914, a number of European powers went to war against Turkey (itself allied, however, with other European powers) but did so in league with the Arabs, who were trying to overthrow the yoke of their fellow Muslims, the Turks. The Islamic world is generally hostile toward Israel, which enjoys much Western support. This support, however, is not monolithic. It is possible that a future war for the Holy Land could involve a coalition of Western powers against Islamic states seeking to destroy the Jews, but the mechanics of such a conflict look dubious. Setting up either coalition would be difficult. Few Western states would willingly fight for Israel. The most likely scenario is that in the event of a fanatical Islamist movement taking over Jordan and Egypt, war might ensue. The United States might intervene to help Israel, mainly to keep Israel from using its atomic bombs. Hence, another war over the Holy Land by adversaries of different religions is indeed possible. This is not the same thing, however, as a death struggle between the Christian and Muslim worlds.

There are countless examples of enemy scanning, but all of them have in common a desire to revert to a time when foreign affairs were simpler and everything could be viewed as a straightforward moral struggle. Such times rarely existed. But this desire alerts us to another chink in the armor, the search for a simple, foreseeable, easily comprehensible world in which short-term solutions can take care of problems: Cruise missile diplomacy—we search for simple solutions.

To be fair, no country is immune to this desire, and it affects leaders and planners as much as it does the "average American." One manifestation of this is the attempt to explain a situation in terms of one variable, or one problem. This type of reasoning came up fairly often in public discussions of the Vietnam war, as in "What went wrong in Vietnam was that . . . " (fill in your own favorite cause of the fiasco). The case of Vietnam may reflect an equally serious problem, one that explains public frustration with the failure to find a single simple solution. This frustration can become intolerable during a long war and may make sustained strategies difficult in a democratic state. In other words, we may lack the will for sustained foreign policy.

That will sound peculiar to anyone who has pondered the trillions of dollars invested in the half-century-long Cold War, which is one of the greatest examples of sustained effort in the history of international affairs. The Cold War, however, involved certain unique circumstances, most notably the continued existence of a power that was publicly and implacably hostile. On the other hand, there is little public enthusiasm for the maintenance of forces in the Persian Gulf, in Bosnia, or in even in Haiti, a country where the American military has spent a good part of this century. Foreign aid spending is even less popular. Sustained foreign policy means that you have to maintain a position through any means necessary because it is in your national interest to do so—and there has to be sufficient trust of the government to let that government make those decisions. The government's ability to make those decisions is hampered by its inefficient structure: There are numerous institutional and interservice rivalries.

The military services are frequently in competition for funding, which means that their advice on strategic doctrine is not as disinterested as it might appear. In the 1950s, for example, the Army and Navy feared that they would lose ground to the Air Force because of the latter's dominance of atomic weapons, while Air Force pilots feared displacement at the hands of missile specialists. This led to a profusion of projects, including one for the launch of intercontinental ballistic missiles from airplanes. Sometimes the techniques for gaining the budgetary edge became comical, as when an aviation magazine in the 1950s published a (false) leak that the Soviet Union had flown a nuclear-powered airplane and that the United States was falling behind (the Soviets did not possess such a thing). This was merely a ploy to gain extra funding. The rivalries elsewhere are more serious. The lack of cooperation among the intelligence offices is legendary. The bad relationship among staff at the State Department and the National Security Council and other White House-controlled entities is equally problematic. Conflicts are not completely bad—they can generate a lot of creative thinking—but they have also been wasteful and have resulted in a lot of bad advice given to administrations. Such a confused capital cannot exercise leadership during the most difficult time of a great power's history. The most difficult time for a great power is when it is declining, and this is now the American situation.

The problem here is not the decline itself, but rather the process of adapting to the decline. Power is never permanent, and all countries are either gaining or losing it at any given moment. The real problem is how a government that is mistrusted, divided, politically chaotic, and poorly organized can lead the country toward some type of new consensus and new foreign policy that will stand the test of time.

On the surface, America does not appear to be declining. It is unquestionably the world's greatest military power and the world's greatest economic power. The decline nevertheless exists, even if it is only relative. As other countries' economies grow and industrialization globalizes, the U.S. share of world economic output will decline, making the world less dependent on economic trends in America. Ultimately this will lead to a reduced role for the American dollar in world trade, which will be extremely costly for Americans. Less subtle aspects of this decline are easier to observe. The United States remains dangerously dependent on foreign oil and other resources, and is also far too dependent on foreign money for private investment and financing the government debt. These problems would be more readily solved and would cause less anxiety if more people understood the inevitable ebb and flow of global power politics. A sense (and knowledge) of history would help America negotiate its global perils.

Some of our lack of historical awareness of the rise and fall of great powers doubtlessly stems from our inability to come to terms with being a great power. Suffice it say that countless nations have experienced and survived these fluctuations, while others have perished. Spain, for example, was Europe's, and arguably the world's, greatest power in 1550, yet a century later its government was bankrupt. Spain survived the collapse but never regained its great-power status, arguably as much due to domestic problems as to factors of foreign policy. Russia rose slowly until it exploded onto the major-power scene under Peter the Great (1689–1725); it began to decline during the Crimean War (1854–1856) and collapsed during the revolution of 1917. Reincarnated as the Soviet Union, it became a superpower, but lost that status with its dissolution in 1991. Russia will be back. Britain governed a quarter of the globe as late as World War II, but the cost of two global wars was too great to sustain its imperial ambitions. It should be noted, however, that Britain still exists, its language and institutions remain global, and it has not experienced a single successful invasion in 930 years.

It is an encouraging example, to say the least. America must find out how to emulate it.

7

WHAT WE CAN DO

National security does not happen by accident—at least, not entirely. True, many nations have survived crises or escaped them completely because of factors over which they had no control, or because of decisions taken by neighbors that they did not even know about. For example, Holland escaped World War I because Germany decided in 1909 to leave its small neighbor unmolested. But Dutch actions had contributed to this German decision. Holland had improved its army and fortifications while signaling its intent to defend itself, establishing that even there a small state was able to protect itself. The United States is in a much better position, militarily and financially, to secure its position and ensure its survival. On the other hand, nations have often undermined their own positions through their actions, and survival means avoiding major errors as well as taking steps to enhance security.

The most difficult thing, especially in an uncertain and unclear period, is for the nation to think about the distant future, not just the immediate present. The choices that are made now will affect the national security and our survival for the next half century. While we look forward to the beginning of the next millennium, we have to think in terms of the year 2050. The reason for this is obvious. While it is impossible to predict exactly what kind of crises will occur in the next fifty years, how well we cope with them will be determined now. The ability of the United States and its allies to survive the next Persian Gulf crisis depends on what we do now to reduce dependence on imported oil. The likelihood of waging and winning a major war is linked to how well we build our armed forces now. Most important, the quality of government decision-making in the future depends on reforms made in the present.

Attempts to solve these problems by means of simple rules are doomed. The complexities of crises, wars, and foreign policy generally nullify all attempts to impose simplistic formulas. None of the sophisticated students of war and crisis have tried to distill their knowledge in that way, although their followers (and detractors) have sometimes pictured their work in terms of a few easy-to-understand rules. Of course, it is the fate of philosophers generally to have their ideas reduced to a few maxims. This is certainly the fate of one of modern history's most famous philosophers of war, Carl von Clausewitz (1780–1831). Even his fellow Prussians interpreted his doctrine of annihilation of the enemy to refer to a gigantic battle of destruction, whereas he makes clear (when read carefully) that imposing one's will on the enemy was enough; destruction was a means to an end, not an end in itself.

The failures of rigid rules of war and rigid ideologies imposed on war are legion. Certainly Hitler's failure in World War II can be traced to his increasing imposition of Nazi ideology on the war effort, substituting fanatical ideas for the realities of the battlefield. This was not immediately apparent when Hitler came to power in 1933, because the Nazi government allowed its military to expand some of its most innovative arms. Nazi ideology soon crippled the flexibility of German strategic thought, however. First, Nazism's conflict-oriented world view demanded that Germany go to war, even though Germany was already the continent's most powerful state. Second, Nazism increasingly evaluated its opponents in racial terms, which contributed to the gross underestimation of Soviet capacity. Finally, Nazism became the foundation of strategic and tactical battlefield decisions, to the point that Hitler even took personal command of a battalion in the war's last year. This ideological rigidity helps explain, for example, why the SS's level of casualties was higher than the army's. Soldiers were ideologically motivated, and many officers were ideologically chosen.

Soviet strategy, while in many ways extremely sophisticated, suffered from attempts to fit all information into a Marxist-Leninist model. The result was less disastrous than in Germany because Marxism does strive to be scientific. While Nazism manufactured facts, Marxism only twisted them. In the Cold War, an effort occurred to make decision-making more scientific. The result was a model of warfare that was peculiar to Western eyes, and hence often misinterpreted. Warfare was reduced to a series of algorithms into which officers were supposed to plug information to determine the "correlation of forces." It will be fascinating to study the extent to which Soviet officers applied this model, whether in peacetime planning or in Afghanistan. Could it, for example, compensate for the Marxist-Leninist state's tendency to centralize all decision-making—or maybe make it worse? The Soviet system could be creative and adaptive, as World War II showed, but the creativity and adaptation surfaced only after the chaos of war had overpowered prewar rigidity.

In the end, Soviet strategy still had to be fitted to an ideological interpretation of world affairs, and this undoubtedly contributed to the Soviet Union's demise. But this kind of thinking was not unique to the Soviet Union. American strategy after 1945 was also hamstrung by a need to force every occurrence into a bipolar, Cold War model, making it impossible for us to understand many events in the so-called Third World and contributing to long-term poor relations with many countries—a problem that will haunt us in the future. On a more practical level, Napoleon's early opponents were defeated because of their rigid adherence to the traditional style of warfare in the eighteenth century, while the great Corsican used flexibility and innovation to overcome them. In turn, Napoleon's interpreters tried to reduce his style of warfare to a set of rules, thereby misunderstanding his achievements and leaving an impoverished intellectual legacy for future strategists.

The most famous example of the difficulty of making simplistic rules, however, can be stated in a single word: Munich. This refers, of course, to the most infamous diplomatic agreement of the twentieth century, an agreement that essentially rewarded Hitler's aggressiveness, encouraged him to take even bigger risks, and prevented the early destruction of the Nazi Reich. The word "appeasement" became a swearword as a result of the Munich agreement.

The facts of the crisis are usually presented as follows: In the summer of 1938, Hitler's Nazi Germany surrounded western Czechoslovakia on three sides. Hitler demanded that Czechoslovakia give him its extreme western region, the Sudetenland, because it contained a high proportion of ethnic Germans. The Sudetenland lay like a horseshoe around western Czechoslovakia, and contained that country's defensive fortifications, as well as much heavy industry and raw materials. Czechoslovakia refused, relying on its military alliance with France. France, in turn, had an alliance with Britain. Rather than fighting, however, British Prime Minister Neville Chamberlain favored appeasement, that is, giving Hitler some concessions to keep him satisfied. Without Britain, France could not fight; without British and French support, Czechoslovakia could not resist. In October 1938 at Munich, a treaty was signed giving Hitler the Sudetenland (the Czechoslovaks were not allowed to be present). A few months later Hitler took the rest of Czechoslovakia, and from that point on World War II was all but inevitable, especially as the Soviet Union no longer took France and Britain's opposition to Hitler seriously, and began to negotiate with Hitler.

The lesson seems easy: Appeasement is bad. Aggressors must be resisted and never given any concessions. Munich influenced a generation of postwar leaders, some genuine believers in the wrongness of the British action, others fearful of the political consequences of appearing weak or cowardly. Even George Bush invoked the memory of Munich during the gulf war of 1990 to 1991. A closer examination reveals a different picture.

The British were wrong to try to appease Hitler, but they were not necessarily wrong to try appeasement. Appeasement by itself was not wrong, but it was used in the wrong situation. If Hitler had been a traditional German statesman (and he was none of those three things), and had he not wanted more than to integrate all Germans into a single state, appeasement might have made sense. Britain had lost a million lives in World War I because of a dispute between Austria and Serbia, and to a Britisher the Sudetenland crisis of 1938 had ominous overtones of the Serbian crisis of 1914. World War I had left Britain weakened and impoverished, and the world destabilized. Avoiding another futile conflict over a dispute deep in Europe appeared to make sense. The British mistake was not a faulty policy choice, but the result of faulty intelligence (the misunderstanding of Hitler).

Many other things contributed to the fiasco. Chamberlain's background was in business, and he applied his business negotiating experience to his relations with Hitler, with disastrous results. More rationally, Chamberlain faced a public deeply opposed to war; certainly Vietnam should make us more sympathetic to the risk of leading a divided country into a conflict. British intelligence was faulty in other ways as well. Germany's military strength was overestimated. The German generals who urged Britain to stand firm were not taken seriously. Britain's (and France's) strategic position in 1938, however, was actually poor. Germany no longer had a large and powerful eastern neighbor that could help Britain and France, because the creation of Poland had interposed a physical barrier between Germany and Russia. The United States had made clear that Britain and France could expect no help, and might not even be able to buy supplies on the American market in case of war. But most of all, Chamberlain simply did not believe Britain was ready for war. Clearly he made the wrong decision in 1938, and his poor reputation is entirely deserved. In his defense, Hitler felt that he had been outmaneuvered at Munich. Hitler wanted war in 1938, and was furious that he could not make it happen. Chamberlain gained breathing space, although it did him little good.

The disastrous outcome of the crisis was not, therefore, the result of appeasement itself. A series of fatal misunderstandings and misinterpretations led to a choice of appeasement that was wrong in that particular crisis. The result does not mean that appeasement is wrong in all situations, or even that the British decision was wrong in every way at the time.

At least Chamberlain understood that he had to consider the "global" picture, not only in the geographical sense of worldwide strategy, but also in terms of thinking about the non-military issues as well. Skilled politician that he was, Chamberlain could hardly ignore British public opinion in formulating strategy. It is all the more peculiar that he appeared blind to the political imperatives driving Nazi strategy. Curiously, he separated Germany's foreign and domestic affairs, but not his own—an error that creeps into American decision-making as well. We tend to assume that foreign decisions stem from rational strategic planning, while we know that our own decisions are messy, complicated, and highly politicized. In truth, everyone's foreign policy is linked to domestic politics, which is one reason that all wars are, in essence, political.

One of the peculiarities of the Vietnam War was the derogation of the conflict as a "political" war, implying that there was a purer alternative somewhere. That this is not so was clearly understood by Clausewitz, who, in his masterpiece *On War,* stated in one of his most famous dicta that "war is the continuation of policy by other means." Domestic politics can be part of this "policy," but other non-military considerations can easily enter the picture. European warfare through the eighteenth century tended to be dynastic, economic, and territorial, the rebellions and civil wars of the pre-modern era being more "political." The French Revolution put politics more firmly on the battlefield, with ideology becoming a major force for war and crisis. This tendency reached its greatest extreme in midcentury when fascism, Nazism, militarism, and communism threatened the established global order through war and revolution. It is no coincidence that the most costly and barbaric war in history was waged between the extremes of Nazism and Stalinist communism (the Russo-German war of 1941–1945).

Happily, ideological fanaticism is on the wane somewhat. Its historical predecessor, religious zealotry, is still very dangerous since it can justify unlimited violence and, even in more stable countries, interfere with rational decision-making. Rational thinking, difficult enough in times of crisis, can be limited even further by ideology and religion. Worse, the outside observer cannot always tell whether policymakers are engaging in "rational" thought. Many observers in the 1930s considered Chamberlain and his predecessor, Baldwin, to be more rational than Churchill, yet the latter had a far better grasp of the nature of the monstrosity that was developing beyond the Rhine. On a more tactical and military level, French military and strategic thought between the wars was entirely rational, and the only criticism that can be leveled at it is that it failed utterly, despite twenty years of preparation. France did make rational plans to protect its security, but that alone was not enough. In other words, future security is not something that can ever be guaranteed.

The French, and the pre-Churchill British leaders, failed because they placed exaggerated reliance on the idea that conflict could be prevented through deterrence and diplomacy. There are several basic reasons that this view, still popular today, is worse than useless at certain times. First, conflict is inherent and inevitable. Conflict does not require a defined set of circumstances; it only requires people. The prevalence of warfare from ancient times to the present demonstrates that conflict, or at least its more peaceable twin, competition, forms an inherent part of human nature. Even if we accept the theories of John Locke, Karl Marx, and Margaret Mead that human behavior is a function of societal and childhood experiences, the sheer volume of conflict-type behavior argues that the conditions that make people conflict-oriented are so prevalent that whether this behavior is truly inherent makes no difference.

This also leads to the conclusion that conflict is inevitable. As discussed earlier, attempting to remove all conditions that create conflict would not only be impossible, but also ineffective. True, heading off economic disasters would remove much of the support for extremist movements. Even that would not convince every nation that its economic wealth, territorial size, and so on were "fair." Conflict— not necessarily war—is bound to ensue. To put it another way,

Perceived injustice lies at the foundation of the international system.

Survival therefore depends on containing conflicts and their causes in such a way that national survival is ensured. This requires, once again, a truly global approach to national security, considering all problems that might threaten the nation, and anticipating trends that are most likely to lead to a catastrophe. Most of all, we need to have the level of knowledge and the level of force to cope with the unexpected.

SURVIVING A DANGEROUS TIME

The historical record of which nations have survived and which have not is too complex to summarize in a single book. Some nations have survived the most appalling policy choices—Germany in the first half of this century comes to mind. The costs of such survival, however, were enormous. Germany is today Europe's most powerful and prosperous state, yet its two great wars cost it enormously, led to the complete occupation and division of the country in 1945, and certainly benefitted the country in no ways whatsoever. At best we can conclude that countries with large populations, cultural unity, and a strong sense of "self" will survive defeat and occupation, but this is hardly a rationale for pursuing risky militaristic policies.

Britain has been more successful at avoiding destruction in war, although it had no more success in keeping its overseas empire than any other country. Geography gave Britain an advantage, but there is more. Britain's approach to foreign affairs has been characterized by a pragmatism and caution that, while it occasionally backfired (as at Munich) has as much to do with Britain's 930 years of freedom from conquest as anything else. Qualitatively, Britain's armed forces were second to none, despite many well-documented failings (as might be expected given their long record). Britain won, or was on the winning side, in the Cold War, World War II, World War I, the wars of the French Revolution (including the War of 1812), and the Anglo-French war that raged alongside the American Revolution. Britain was successful at maintaining alliances when necessary, dividing its potential adversaries, and using its geographical advantage to enter wars and project force when necessary. Freedom of action was thereby maintained. Whether Britain can survive the forces of devolution (country-dividing) that are so powerful in our time remains to be seen. It would be ironic, but not without precedent, if a country that has been so extraordinarily successful at repelling external threats fell prey to internal dissension.

Britain's ability to remain flexible in the face of global instability is one point that is particularly relevant to the American posture. America's economic and military power has produced a tendency to take inflexible positions at times in international affairs without much attention to local factors or the sensitivities and sensibilities of the locals. This tendency has been enhanced by the "lesson" of the Munich agreement—that appeasement is inherently bad. A flexible posture can still be combined with the other behavioral factors needed to survive global instability: strength, determination, and unity of purpose. Military strength is obviously indispensable. Determination to survive and to protect key interests is not inconsistent with maintenance of a flexible strategic posture. Unity of purpose, sometimes referred to as national unity, is essential to survive the setbacks that will inevitably come in the next century. In fact, some of those setbacks may not be survivable, in a strategic sense. Only unity of purpose can lead a once-defeated nation to enable it to rebuild itself. Unlike Germany, the United States as a whole has never had to deal with this particular conundrum (although the South has).

As established earlier, aggregate military strength alone will not guarantee the desired outcome. The national military establishment must have three characteristics. First, it must be flexible enough to adapt when circumstances change. Second, the cohesion of the military must be maintained by taking steps to retain high morale, even in adverse circumstances. Third, the military must be neither so strong nor so weak as to create an attraction for aggressors. (The "weakness" side of this is obvious, but a country that is militarily too strong attracts enmity and opposition, as happened to Germany in 1890–1914.)

No strategic doctrine or military establishment will be successful unless it is understood, as taught by various strategists, that war is essentially a psychological struggle waged with physical means. Force alone will prevail in neither crisis nor war; instead, a combination of intelligence and will is needed, both during a crisis or war, and even more important in the period before a crisis or war when preparation is still possible.

Accordingly, the following steps must be taken for us to be able to cope with these dangerous times:

Recommendation 1. INTENSIVE PUBLIC EDUCATION IN INTERNATIONAL AFFAIRS

Foreign and military policy in inseparable from public opinion, especially over the long run. A knowledgeable public is absolutely essential if the nation is going to survive dangerous times. Otherwise, irrational reactions may occur.

Recommendation 2. UNIVERSAL MILITARY TRAINING

The draft would have three advantages. First, it would give the country, in times of crisis, a much bigger military establishment, and the presence of mobilizeable military units around the country could be used to cope with disaster and to maintain national cohesion. An elite, high-tech, professional army is unbeatable—on the first day of a war. Each day thereafter, its advantage degrades as its experienced soldiers are killed, and if there are no large reserves to replace them, defeat becomes inevitable. In addition, having a large army allows for simultaneously meeting many different commitments (although whether all those commitments should be kept shall be addressed later). Second, the military could become a means to inculcate civics and citizenship, by giving people a shared experience of service under the American flag. Third, service would give the public more awareness regarding military issues.

Recommendation 3. SUPPORT NON-REPRESSIVE CULTURAL UNITY

No strategic threat exceeds that of internal disunity. The United States has absorbed immigrant populations and will continue to do so. Nevertheless, separatism—especially linguistic separatism—must be discouraged, but not through repressive means. A hostile repressed population adds no strength whatsoever. In fact, the most dangerous threat to national security is the possibility of a separatist movement developing among the Chicano population in the Southwest. Such a movement currently exists only among fringe intellectuals and college students, but that does not mean that it will remain that way. This threat must be headed off now, in a non-repressive fashion. Illegal immigration must be slowed to a level that the country can comfortably absorb. In addition, the government should make English-language programs freely available to all those who desire them, when and where they are desired. The immigrant population must be assimilated, but through *amistad* (friendship), not force.

History abounds with examples of societies destroyed through internal disunity, be it along racial, ethnic, or class lines. The Assyrian Empire attempted to rule its disparate peoples through repression and was, not surprisingly, destroyed by them. The Roman Empire was never able to make peace between its established citizenry and the large numbers of "barbarians" who settled within its boundaries. The Mongols could defeat all opponents, but could not develop a political system that could tie the many "Mongol" peoples together in a long-lasting whole. The Austrian Empire was unable to build a political structure acceptable to its many minorities and perished. Canada may yet collapse if Quebec decides to depart. The United States survived its most disunited moment—the Civil War—but suffered more fatalities than in the two world wars combined. Clearly, both repression and the more divisive forms of multiculturalism should be avoided.

Recommendation 4. ENSURE FISCAL STABILITY

Economic wealth and military security do not precisely correlate, but a fiscal collapse could undermine the country's stability, as well its ability to maintain military forces. Therefore, the government should take steps to put both private and public sector finances in order and to maintain the stability of the dollar. In the public sector, this means an immediate halt to deficit spending (at least in times of prosperity, something the country can easily afford), and placing limits on indefinite expansion of spending (by abolishing cost-of-living allowances, for example). In the private sector, this should take the effect of discouraging the assumption of excessive debt, perhaps by placing limits on interest deductibility. Finally, banking systems are so globally interconnected that the collapse of one system can easily rebound in a matter of hours into other countries (including ours), and steps need to be taken to prevent this from causing a crisis. At the very least, liquidity requirements need to be sufficient to head off such a disaster.

Recommendation 5. PREPARE FOR POST-CRISIS OR POSTWAR SURVIVAL

A major economic or fiscal crisis or a limited nuclear war could leave the country in complete chaos. At the least, the government needs to stockpile critical supplies in every region of the country, and have military units available to administer areas (especially after a nuclear strike), and to maintain order.

Recommendation 6. STRESS POLITICAL UNITY

Disunity is a cherished American tradition that worked fairly well when the country was isolated and unthreatened, and when the country was so strong that foreign threats were irrelevant. Neither of these situations exists anymore. Promoting unity without discouraging vigorous debate is difficult; McCarthyite situations need to be avoided at all costs. In foreign affairs, however, there needs to be a middle ground. Furthermore, voters must discourage politicians from taking foreign policy positions demanded by a single ethnic or pressure group.

SURVIVING THE MOMENT OF DANGER

Making it through a crisis involves three surprisingly different tasks. The first, obviously, is foreseeing. This is not easy, as a foreseeable crisis is almost a contradiction in terms. True, obvious flashpoints exist around the globe, but even if the location can be predicted, the timing cannot (unless you are initiating the crisis, of course). The Cold War had gone on for seventeen years before the Cuban Missile Crisis, yet both powers had to stumble through the crisis and barely extricated themselves without damage. The second task is crisis prevention. Peace and security agreements and foreign aid are the typical tools for this task, although more extreme measures, such as overthrowing a potentially hostile government, could also be included. The third task, which we are focusing on here, is surviving the crisis itself.

There are two typical types of international crises, each with its own pitfalls. The first type is a confrontation with another state. As this kind of crisis can be handled through direct negotiation, making and responding to threats, and so on, there are fairly conventional procedures for limiting the escalation of such a crisis. The greatest danger in such a crisis is that the decision parameters—the self-imposed rules—of the foreign government may be unknown, misunderstood, or may change in the middle of the crisis.

The second type of crisis is the outflow of an economic collapse. This is far more dangerous because such a crisis stimulates fanatical political parties (and sometimes religious movements) with which negotiations are difficult, perhaps impossible; they are difficult because in an unstable political movement no one has the power in that movement to make a binding agreement, and may be impossible because a true fanatical movement does not change its goals except when it is destroyed. Such a crisis causes systems to collapse and creates so many imponderables that survival becomes acutely difficult. The most obvious example of this is World War II, when economic instability (and other problems) strengthened radical movements in Germany, southern Europe, and Japan. The problem is not new, however. The Congress of Vienna (1814–1815) was responding to precisely this risk of revolution-inspired war and violence.

The position of the United States in relation to crises has changed enormously in the last half century. Until World War II, the illusion of possible non-involvement remained. The war and the subsequent Cold War educated many, however temporarily, that the United States was not immune to global trends. Geography proved to be an illusory advantage, especially as the United States acquired military commitments in every corner of the globe. The defensive frontier of the United States was moved (quite openly) from California and Maine to Asia and Europe. Had crises erupted simultaneously in several places, America would have been unable to keep its commitments and would have probably used nuclear weapons to salvage the situation—with fateful results.

Political divisions during a crisis can be catastrophic, especially if they prevent the government from acting in the way it sees fit. This became especially obvious during the Iranian hostage crisis when President Carter, under great political pressure, sought to liberate the hostages through military force, despite advice from his secretary of state that the mission was a bad idea. The rescue effort crashed and burned, and so did Carter. On the other hand, vigorous debate about foreign policy is not a bad thing. In fact, the impact of political unity in crisis is mixed. The following table lists four prominent crises in the last sixty years, two of which provoked unity, while the two others created division:

CRISIS	POLITICAL SITUATION	OUTCOME
Cuban Missile	Unity: Bipartisan support	Positive: crisis ends satisfactorily for U.S.A.
Gulf of Tonkin	Unity: Only two senators vote against resolution authorizing Lyndon Johnson to act	Negative: The information about attack was inaccurate, and Vietnam War escalates

CRISIS	POLITICAL SITUATION	OUTCOME
Hitler's aggression	Division: Churchill attacks Baldwin-Chamberlain appeasement policies	Positive: Churchill was right and his attacks informed the public of the dangers ahead
Iran hostage	Division: Carter under vigorous pressure to act	Negative: Carter vacillated from one policy to another, and wound up up approving a disastrous rescue attempt

The record is mixed. Political divisions can, however, clearly have an adverse impact in a crisis that is often overlooked during our vigorous political debates: Foreigners read newspapers too. The sometimes overheated rhetoric of the American campaign trail resonates somewhat strangely when read in foreign lands, and can easily be misinterpreted. Second, in an attempt to gain electoral advantage, a crisis may be exploited by unscrupulous politicians who thereby create waves of national paranoia that injure the body politic and do nothing at all for national security (this happened after both world wars, for example). Instead, political leaders and citizens need to encourage the government to engage in the three tactics suggested earlier to survive a crisis: enhance inherent advantages, exploit mistakes, and make broad and flexible preparations.

Accordingly, in addition to Recommendations 1 and 2 (intensive public education on international affairs and universal military training) mentioned above, the following steps need to be taken to survive the moment of danger:

Recommendation 7. LIMIT GLOBAL COMMITMENTS

Foreign commitments through military alliances should never exceed two often confused criteria. First, commitments should never exceed the national capacity to meet them. Second, commitments should never exceed the national will to meet them. Few things are as dangerous as commitments that surpass either of these criteria, because they can provoke confusion in the midst of a crisis and lead to panic and excessive escalation, or undignified and dangerous withdrawals, perhaps causing other allies to doubt our will and ability.

Recommendation 8. AVOID ISOLATIONISM

In the wake of an era of enormous overcommitment and high-risk policies, it is understandable that some would like to return to an era when the United States could withdraw from world affairs; this is simply impossible and, as discussed earlier, would create more risks, not fewer.

Recommendation 9. INSTITUTIONALIZE OUTSIDE ANALYSIS OF INTELLIGENCE

Nothing is as important in a crisis as good information. Unfortunately, bureaucratic politics, groupthink, and a desire to please the recipient of the information create anomalies in the flow of intelligence. Two ways of dealing with this problem are: (1) bringing in outsiders (academics, knowledgeable journalists, etc.) to analyze intelligence information; and (2) rotating analysts regularly among the different national security bureaucracies.

Recommendation 10. AVOID OVERHEATED RHETORIC

There is no specific way of forcing politicians to restrict the use of inflammatory and irresponsible language, unless public education succeeds in creating an electorate that knows why such language is so dangerous.

Recommendation 11. INSTITUTIONALIZE BIPARTISANSHIP

Especially in times of crisis, it is necessary to bring the leadership of the opposition party (the party that does not control the White House) inside the corral, which may help with Recommendation 10 since knowledge brings a kind of complicity with the final decisions. Two ways exist to bring this about: (1) Give top congressional leaders access to secrets as a matter of law; and (2) place opposition leaders on the National Security Council.

Recommendation 12. MAINTAIN FORCE PROJECTION CAPABILITY

This has been America's military trump card for some time, essentially the British Empire's methods on a much larger scale. It is a very expensive capability, and more efficient ways of ferrying forces to far-away places will have to be investigated. Heavily protected and armored troop transports will be necessary soon because (1) air superiority is not going to be a given in every situation; (2) air superiority is not going to suppress all opposition fire; and (3) the aircraft carrier is a premier target as well as a premier weapon; sooner or later one will be sunk, and the investment in a single warship of that size may become prohibitive.

Recommendation 13. ENCOURAGE PUBLIC CALMNESS

This may seem like a function of Recommendation 10. In reality, the government should be prepared to engage in intensive communications with the public to put the crisis in perspective and prevent mass panic. Public education in international affairs, discussed in the previous section, would be invaluable.

Recommendation 14. LEAVE THE ADVERSARY AN EXIT

As mentioned earlier, Sun Tzu emphasized that in every conflict the enemy should be given a way out. There were two reasons behind this suggestion, one applicable only to war, the other more to crisis. In war, a retreating army becomes disorganized and vulnerable, so that allowing an opening for retreat may lead to a more total victory. More relevant is Sun Tzu's observation, proved so often in practice, that an enemy forced to fight to the death will do much more damage to you than an enemy given an honorable way to depart the field.

This is not meant to suggest that the Allies in World War II made a mistake when, at Casablanca, they demanded an "unconditional surrender" from the Axis powers. Sun Tzu's dictum was designed for an opponent who would attempt to withdraw, which Hitler certainly would not. In 1941, he correctly sensed that a withdrawal from Moscow would expose his army to greater losses than if it stayed stuck in the snow. In addition, Sun Tzu's suggestion was also designed to conserve your own forces. Such forces would then be available to deal with a third and subsequent opponents. In the bipolar Axis-U.N. struggle, this was not a factor until the Cold War loomed. By 1945, however, the U.N. forces did not have to concern themselves much about conserving personnel, except perhaps in the case of the Soviet Union. The Nazi-Soviet struggle was a true fight without quarter, however, so that conserving strength was something that the Soviet Union really could not consider.

How does this recommendation apply to modern crises? Paradoxically, by focusing on how we may survive a crisis, we have omitted the rather obvious fact that often both sides have to survive if one is going to. In other words, giving an adversary no face-saving means of settling a crisis leaves that adversary with exactly two choices: humiliation or war. Surviving a crisis demands understanding and occasionally, strangely enough, helping an opponent.

SURVIVAL THROUGH PREPARATION

How well prepared a nation is for crisis and war depends on inherent advantages, which cannot be changed, and long-term trends, which are difficult to spot and even more difficult to affect. Mistakes by an adversary can offset shortcomings in preparations, but such mistakes can cause trouble for both combatants. For example, a mistake during a nuclear confrontation might involve launching nuclear missiles when it is not strategically necessary. This enemy mistake hardly benefits the bombed party. Relying on others' mistakes is not only hopelessly optimistic, but can be dangerous.

The United States has an obvious advantage and an obvious disadvantage when it comes to preparation. The obvious advantage is that the country's wealth, power, and size give it the resources to support preparation. However, these same things also increase the country's vulnerability, however. Size and wealth give us more to protect, while power attracts opposition ("countervailing power") and resentment.

Protecting America through preparation is therefore a complex process, requiring the development of systems that are sufficiently strong and flexible to meet threats that cannot be foreseen. General strategic steps must include keeping our deployment or force projection capability intact, engaging in risk reduction, formulating an economic strategy, building political support, and engaging in diplomacy aimed both at foreign governments and foreign peoples.

To an extent, all these things happened during the Cold War when America waged the conflict on both political and military levels, achieving some success on both. Cold War strategy worked for two reasons. First, it was understood from the beginning that the Cold War was primarily a political struggle; and second, World War II had prepared America militarily and politically. America inherited from the war an experienced civil-military bureaucracy and a huge pool of military talent, not to mention an immense quantity of technology. Although the United States won (or the Stalinist forces lost, depending on one's interpretation), some obvious problems surfaced during the Cold War, problems linked more to thinking than fighting. The large, insulated, heavily bureaucratized national security apparatus fostered an inflexible, simplistic world view permitting too few nuances. This did not matter greatly at the time, but in the modern multipolar world, such thinking could be fatal.

In sum, American strategic preparation must achieve the following: The military must be able to mobilize quickly, sustain a war effort, and, when diplomats require, make threats. Friends must be kept through alliances with governments and foreign aid aimed at building ties with the people. Risk reduction must be secured by reducing imports and analyzing our commitments to hot spots (likely places of confrontation) and warm spots (where revolutions could occur). Improvements in decision-making should foster bipartisanship, centralization without discouraging flexibility, and retention of freedom of action. The specific steps to bring this about are: Recommendation 2 (universal military training); Recommendation 5 (prepare for post-crisis or postwar survival); Recommendation 7 (limit commitments); Recommendation 9 (institutionalize outside analysis of intelligence); Recommendation 11 (institutionalize bipartisanship); Recommendation 12 (maintain force projection capability); as well as the following:

Recommendation 15. PROMOTE BRITISH INTERESTS

Britain's economic and political health are not luxuries for the United States. While the United States has been more a Pacific than an Atlantic power for the last century, the alliance with Britain has been such an integral part of modern American foreign policy that its loss would destabilize U.S. foreign policy. In addition, geography and political principles make Britain and America natural allies. Particularly at a time when Britain is threatened with devolution, the United States should take steps to strengthen the British position. Any economic or political incentives to Scotland to stop the devolutionary movement would be a good investment.

Recommendation 16. LOWER OUR INTERNATIONAL PROFILE

Our tendency to take high-profile positions in every crisis, to insist on taking the lead in every military and political alliance, and to speak frequently, publicly, and aggressively on every major issue brings us no benefits (except some domestic political ones). The global leadership role cannot be abandoned but should be exercised quietly and cautiously. In particular, the current regular and formal public meddling in foreign governments' affairs, through certifying countries' drug policies and analyzing every other country's human rights record in the annual State Department report, must come to an immediate end. There are times that such meddling is useful, but the current practice of legally requiring the government to issue such reports allows for no strategic or diplomatic considerations of whether they ought to be issued at all.

Recommendation 17. EXPAND FOREIGN AID SPENDING

Our foreign aid budget is much smaller than most Americans believe. The typical figure accounts for less than 1 percent of total federal spending, and most of it is military aid and aid to a very small group of countries (Israel and Egypt being the largest recipients by far). Foreign aid is a strategic weapon, even when the motives behind it are charitable. At the very least, foreign aid is a cheap way of convincing others that we are generous, which has long-term political benefits. More important, foreign aid can create alliances, friendships, and, if given to a hostile country, dependence. Finally, substantial foreign aid spending can head off the kind of economic crisis that could cause the whole international system to collapse and plunge the world into a series of costly and bloody wars.

Recommendation 18. PARTIAL AUTARKY

Autarky is the concept of having a completely self-sufficient economy that is dependent on no other country for its needs. Complete autarky is neither possible nor healthy, but partial autarky would give the United States more flexibility in a crisis. In practice, there are three things that could be done to bring this about: stockpiling natural resources, imposing a gas tax to reduce oil consumption, and the construction of new nuclear plants to reduce energy dependence— and also to prepare the country for the day when the oil and natural gas begin to run out.

SURVIVAL THROUGH FREEDOM OF ACTION

Freedom of action was defined earlier as the ability to make a legitimate choice that is not forced upon you. A legitimate choice is one that is neither irrational nor suicidal. The forcing can be done by an adversary or by circumstances. Freedom of action, then, boils down to the retention of flexibility, and this means that it is the opposite of overextension. Once a nation's forces are overextended, all freedom of action has been lost. Freedom of action cannot exist without some form of preparation.

What kind of preparation? Earlier, we saw that having more military force than an adversary was no guarantee of success. There were five reasons for this: The smaller power may have allies; the location of the conflict may favor the smaller power; the style of warfare may favor the smaller power; the greater power may have other commitments; and it may face limitations on its use of force due to political and diplomatic reasons. Yet a larger military does provide one key advantage: It provides more options in a crisis. This is exactly why John F. Kennedy supported military expansion; he did not want to be forced to use nuclear weapons. A large military does not guarantee victory, but it does increase freedom of action. Of course, this freedom of action can be abused, as the military might be overused, misused (Vietnam), or even used to start a conflict, which is a very poor use of freedom of action. In fact, freedom of action is at the same time so valuable and so ephemeral that it is absolutely dependent on the correctness and timing of decisions taken by the government.

Can freedom of action belong to only participants in a crisis or war? It can belong to more, but this is not a stable or lasting situation. For one thing, the greater the adversary's freedom of action, the more circumscribed is your own. Furthermore, if you are seeking some type of victory, there are two things you will do that will limit freedom of action. First, you will use your own resources and take initiatives, which over time will reduce your freedom of action. Second, in order to secure your position and undermine your adversary's, you will take all possible steps to eliminate his or her freedom of action.

In other words, the dynamic of a conflict operates to eliminate freedom of action on both sides, with the advantage belonging to the side that retains its freedom of action longer.[23] To retain our freedom of action, Recommendation 2 (universal military training) should be implemented. This significantly increases options in a crisis. Recommendation 6 (stress political unity) is important because domestic political discord can lead

23. Sun Tzu's dictum concerning leaving the enemy a way out clearly applies to freedom of action. Denying the adversary all freedom of action leaves him or her little opportunity but to fight—and escalate. It would not apply, however, if the adversary had already escalated or indicated that he would, regardless, as in the case of Hitler.

to decisional paralysis, eliminating all freedom of action. Recommendations 7 (limit commitments) and 12 (maintain force projection) are important to ensure freedom of action, as is Recommendation 14, because eliminating the adversary's freedom of action completely, can lead to suicidal counterattacks. Partial autarky (Recommendation 18) would allow the United States to contemplate carefully whether or not to go to war with an atomic Ayatollah.

Recommendation 19. STRENGTHEN THE FORCES FOR PEACE

Soviet military thought stressed that wars were avoided by the presence of "forces for peace," that is, tendencies within a country to avoid war, rather than because of the impact of deterrence. This view stems from Marxist thought and the experience of World War II, in which the Soviet Union faced a nation that could not have been deterred. A major war, or simultaneous smaller wars or crises, could eliminate America's freedom of action very quickly. Support for the forces for peace (countries and political movements less inclined to use violence and aggression) would be a good investment. Unfortunately, the dividing line between supporting such forces and active meddling in someone else's domestic affairs is thin, and in some cases nonexistent, and such actions would have to be done in the greatest secrecy.

Recommendation 20. EMERGENCY PREPARATIONS FOR SELF-SUFFICIENCY

As discussed in Recommendation 18, total autarky is impractical. Nevertheless, the chance of a major interruption of the natural resource flow is real. A workable plan needs to be prepared allowing the nation to function for a year or two without, for example, oil imports.

Recommendation 21. KEEP THE BOMB

While the strategic direct benefits of nuclear weapons are rather limited, such weapons do limit an adversary's freedom of action.

DECIDING FOR SURVIVAL

Rules and principles interfere with quality decision-making if they are used as rigid formulas rather than as general guidelines. Another benefit of knowing fundamental principles of war and conflict is that they can act as stimuli to thinking. One can read Clausewitz, Jomini, Liddell Hart, Miksche, and so on, and learn without necessarily agreeing with everything they said. Mistakes in formulating national strategy arise more from errors in the way of thinking than from choosing the wrong strategic principle. The Vietnam War is an example of this, especially because of the confusion that existed in Washington between imposing one's will and imposing one's way of war. The latter (bombing) was confused with the former (winning).

For this reason, how decisions are made is more important than what decisions are to be made or how they are to be carried out. These modes of decision-making were identified earlier as types 2, 1, and 3, respectively. Type 1 (what decisions are to be made) is essential, if only because it compels government to contemplate the future and consider the problems that will have to be faced. In reality, however, plans all too often are out of phase with the reality of the situation in which they have to be used, if only because of changing technology and the inherent unpredictability of world affairs. Worse, inappropriate Type 1 plans will still dominate discussions during a crisis because of the inherent dominance of an existing plan, and the dangerous tendency to substitute planning for thinking. Type 1's greatest benefit, however, may be as a means of generating bipartisan support on major issues. During the Cold War, for example, most arguments were over means (type 3) rather than ends.

Type 3 (how plans are to be carried out) deals with technical matters. Technical planning can cause severe problems, however, if it impinges on the formation of national policy and strategy. Under no circumstances should type 3 planning "drive" the others. The most notorious example of this occurred in 1914 when the German Schlieffen Plan led Germany to invade France and Belgium before it was strategically necessary.[24]

Decision-making depends on accurate observation and analysis. This is especially difficult in international affairs because of the problems of cross-cultural misunderstandings and the fact that governments are habitually secretive. It becomes even more difficult in times of crisis,

---

24. The Schlieffen Plan can be interpreted differently. Schlieffen's plan did represent two important parts of Germany's policy; namely, its paranoia regarding its neighbors and its belief that France would stab it in the back if Germany went to war with Russia.

because time for gathering and analyzing information is so short. In wartime, when chaos rules, all decisions are knowingly based on inaccurate and incomplete information. Philosophers have long struggled with the fact that even under ideal circumstances, our ability to observe is limited. In crisis and war, the difficulties are magnified and hence survival depends on exceptional skills in type 2 decision-making.

Type 2 planning can take change into account but can be crippled by inflexibility or chaos. These two risks are built into the current decision-making structure. The Constitution gives the president great power in foreign and military affairs but does little to clarify how decisions are to be made. The war-making powers of the presidency are not defined by the Constitution, which merely states that the president shall be commander in chief of the armed forces. Underneath the president is a Cabinet, but as a body, it has no constitutional standing (in fact, it is not mentioned in the Constitution) and Cabinet officers today have less authority in relation to the president than in the past, thanks to the growth of the Cabinet and the profusion of agencies that exist outside the Cabinet structure. The most senior Cabinet position, secretary of state, is but a constitutional shadow of its pre-World War II self. Each agency has its own agenda, as does each branch of the service. These organizations battle through the media, leaking facts (and sometimes lies) that bolster their positions.

Solutions to these problems have to avoid some obvious pitfalls. Proposals that fall afoul of the Constitution accomplish nothing. Excessive centralization might produce inflexibility, while too little could perpetuate chaos. A completely non-political approach (i.e., leaving decisions to small groups of experts) is not practical over the long run, not only because the public would not trust such a system, but because the military's firepower has definite political implications.

The following recommendations for improvements in decision- making have therefore been chosen with some caution. These include Recommendation 1 (intensive public education in international affairs) and Recommendation 6 (stress political unity). Institutionalizing outside analysis of intelligence (Recommendation 9) could be accomplished by rotating analysts among national security bureaucracies, and bringing in journalists, academics, and so on to examine the documents. Decision-making would also benefit from institutionalizing bipartisanship (Recommendation 11) and keeping the Bomb (Recommendation 21). The bomb remains insurance against the failure of policy.

Recommendation 22. A PERMANENT INTERSERVICE GENERAL STAFF

A general staff is the "brains" of an army. It is composed of the officers who write doctrine and plans. Officers would remain with the general staff for the rest of their careers after appointment, although they would rotate through field assignments with the individual services. Promotions would be determined by the general staff, not the individual service. Such a body, which would incorporate interservice agencies such as the Defense Intelligence Agency, would create a team of officers whose perspective would be more genuinely all-service than those whose careers were tied exclusively to a single service. Occasional assignments to operations with other services would be a bonus.

Recommendation 23. STRENGTHEN THE STATE DEPARTMENT

No agency has suffered as much during the Cold War as the State Department. Its budget, large in absolute terms, is minuscule compared with those of other Cold War bureaucracies. In terms of decision-making, it is overshadowed by executive agencies like the National Security Council (NSC). The quality of its work was greatly hampered by the McCarthy-era "investigations." The State Department should regain its former authority by placing the secretary of state clearly in command of all foreign policy decisions, second only to the president, and possibly by placing the CIA and the NSC under the State Department, or at least under the secretary of state.

Recommendation 24. SUPPRESS THE NSC-STATE DEPARTMENT RIVALRY

If the NSC remains a separate, White House entity, the president must ensure an absence of rivalry between it and the State Department. Creative tension should not lead to the existence of competing foreign policies, as happened during the Carter administration.

SURVIVING CHINKS IN THE ARMOR

America's superpower status is not likely to be questioned in the near future, at least from abroad. Such a challenge would require both huge resources and global ambition. At home, the uncertainties of our foreign policy, and the historical ambiguities felt about our role, may well undermine global status before a reduced posture becomes a strategic necessity. A changing and unclear position, however, results in uncertain military strategy, which in turn raises problems with how many troops there ought to be, what weapons should be purchased, and so on. The military may generate elegant and sophisticated models of the future, but these may not be relevant in the absence of a long-term consensus.

We can agree, I believe, on some of the features of our country that make us vulnerable. America's immensely rich and sophisticated economy is a source of vulnerability as well as a source of strength. A poor society can absorb stunning disasters and continue to wage war because its economy is so basic that, paradoxically, disasters do not destroy it. Property losses little affect the poor peasant who has none, and loss of life is much more an accepted feature of daily existence. Not so with us. A great disaster could cause a collapse of morale that might, without preparation, destroy the country. In addition, wealth itself can make a country a target.

Technology is also a double-edged sword. High-tech weaponry dominates the modern battlefield and provides Americans with unparalleled access to information, contributing also to our wealth. Technology, however, also creates strategic vulnerability. People expect technology to supersede the need for blood, and morale could fall precipitously if loss of life approached historical levels. In addition, our dependence on all this technology makes our way of life very vulnerable to its disruption. A single atomic explosion could cripple a large proportion of our communications and our computers, due to the so-called EMP (electromagnetic pulse) effect. Disruptions of oil flow, electricity, and so on could force tremendous economic shutdowns.

A more subtle problem arises from our uncertainty about being a world power. To reconcile this with being a moral (or at least moralistic) country, Americans prefer to see their foreign interventions as crusades, not as *realpolitik*. Up to a point this can be helpful: Support for NATO and the alliance with Israel would never have lasted as long if Americans were solely pragmatic about their world affairs. In an uncertain time, however, the attempt to look for new moral dividing lines does no good. If anything, it makes American foreign policy more unpredictable at the very time that traditional alliances are breaking down. The Israeli alliance is in danger of fracturing; NATO will remain, but its future is cloudy, especially regarding what it is supposed to do, whom it is supposed to oppose, and what members' mutual requirements are.[25]

Not surprisingly, a segment of the American population would prefer a withdrawal—a feeling with both moral and pragmatic justifications. Unfortunately, as demonstrated earlier, the only way that the United States could stop policing the world would be to police the world. Isolationism is not as impractical as its strongest detractors make out, but it can work only if its advocates are willing to pay the price; isolationism could cost more, not less, and would require a drastic reduction in oil consumption, one way or another.

Isolationism is stronger among the public than among the ruling elite, but that does not reduce its significance. Our foreign policy has always been intensely sensitive to public opinion, and this is even more true because of our biennial House elections. These elections had surprisingly little effect on Cold War foreign policy, however, because of the broad public consensus that fighting communism was a good thing. In the absence of such consensus, public mood swings about foreign policy will become greater and have more impact.

This has considerable import in the area of "enemy scanning." Many people, when thinking of America's security, ask: Who are our enemies? Oddly enough, this is not the right question. The correct question is: Which of our behaviors, or which global trends, are going to drag us into the next war? None of the four great twentieth-century American wars began as attacks on the United States. World War I began as a European conflict that America joined on its own initiative in 1917. In World War II, the Axis powers sought land and resources, and Axis member Japan attacked the United States only because America opposed Japanese aggression in Asia. Japan would have been perfectly content to pursue its regional Asian ambition without going to war with us. The Korean War began because the dictator of North Korea wanted the entire peninsula for himself. The Vietnam War began because Ho Chi Minh and his party wanted a unified Vietnam free of foreign powers. In none of those four cases was the United States in any way the primary target of enemy aggression, yet they led to an American war effort requiring seventeen years and 600,000 fatalities.

Many other things interfere as well with the creation of workable

---

25. Paradoxically, NATO has chosen this very moment to expand. At a time that the alliance is already unstable, it is making itself less stable.

foreign policy and military strategy. Frustration with the complexities of international affairs have led to a preference for "Cruise missile diplomacy," the search for simple solutions (an attitude in no way unique to America, although the tendency is not quite as strong in Europe). Maintaining a credible and sustained foreign policy requires a will to do so; do we have it? Interservice and interagency rivalrics damage all policymaking efforts. Our relative decline as a world power creates frustration and makes making choices imperative but more difficult. Finally, the lack of understanding of the historical context of world events creates a shallow dialogue about international affairs—and not just among the mass of the people.

The cure for this situation includes Recommendation 1 (intensive public education on international affairs). People here need to know that a large part of the international order is our creation. In addition, a highly politicized foreign policy is dangerous if voters are not familiar with international affairs, especially if it causes popular demands for simple solutions. Recommendation 2 (universal military training) must be implemented because the potentially short-lived nature of the professional army is a vulnerability in and of itself. Limiting global commitments (Recommendation 7) would take our relative decline into account without turning to isolationism. Recommendation 11 (institutionalize bipartisanship) is essential, given the politicized nature of foreign policy debate today.

Recommendation 12 (maintain force projection) is vital, but with some modification. The type of force projection will have to change. First, many future actions will be police actions for which the traditional high visibility, high firepower mission is not suited. Second, the carrier battle group is potentially very vulnerable, and the loss of a single carrier could have a catastrophic effect on public morale. Fortunately, this is an area in which the Pentagon is making progress, by developing an armored vessel with stealth capability to bring troops and weapons to enemy shores. We will also reduce our vulnerability by lowering our international profile (Recommendation 16) and developing partial autarky (Recommendation 18).

Recommendation 25. ACT AS PART OF ALLIANCES

Although this does reduce freedom of action somewhat, alliances can compensate for numerous vulnerabilities.

Recommendation 26. DEVELOP GREATER COMPUTER AND ELECTRONIC SECURITY

Computers, electronic data systems, and their records are the glue that hold our economic system together.

CONCLUSION

Many years ago, economics was named the "dismal" science because it seemed to offer no hope for improving the future. History, and particularly the history of conflict, may yet steal this epithet from economics. Happily, the record also shows that nations can survive even fearful disasters. Even better, some countries have managed to avoid disaster despite proximity to and participation in great conflicts. Britain, our great friend, has not faced a successful invasion attempt since the year 1066. China survived invasions, incursions, and pressure from Mongols, Russians, many Europeans, Americans, and the Japanese, but parlayed its massive population and cultural strengths into a modern position of great power. India survived nine centuries of occupations by various Muslim rulers, the conquest by the Moghuls, and two centuries of British domination. Most impressive perhaps is the record of Russia, which singlemindedly fought every adversary over the centuries to remain a great state.[26]

Whether America joins these survivors depends on what we do now.

---

26. During the Gorbachev era, Edvard Shevardnadze, the Soviet foreign minister (and later president of Georgia), remarked that he was going to do something terrible to America: he was going to deprive us of an enemy. As discussed earlier, Shevardnadze was wrong. It is Russia that has fared best when facing a great enemy.

APPENDIX

RECOMMENDATIONS

1. Intensive public education in international affairs.
2. Universal military training.
3. Support non-repressive cultural unity.
4. Ensure fiscal stability.
5. Prepare for post-crisis or postwar survival.
6. Stress political unity.
7. Limit global commitments.
8. Avoid isolationism.
9. Institutionalize outside analysis of intelligence.
10. Avoid overheated rhetoric.
11. Institutionalize bipartisanship.
12. Maintain force projection capability.
13. Encourage public calmness.
14. Leave the adversary an exit.
15. Promote British interests.
16. Lower our international profile.
17. Expand foreign aid spending.
18. Partial autarky.
19. Strengthen the forces for peace.
20. Emergency preparations for self-sufficiency.
21. Keep the Bomb.
22. A permanent interservice general staff.
23. Strengthen the State Department.
24. Suppress the NSC-State Department rivalry.
25. Act as part of alliances.
26. Develop greater computer and electronic security.

RECOMMENDATIONS BY TOPIC

Rec. #	Dangerous Time	Moment of Danger	Preparation	Freedom of action	Deciding	Chinks in the armor
1.	x	x				x
2.	x	x	x	x	x	x
3.	x					
4.	x					
5.	x		x			
6.	x			x	x	
7.		x	x	x		x
8.		x				
9.		x	x		x	
10.		x				
11.		x	x		x	x
12.		x	x	x		x
13.		x				
14.		x		x		
15.			x			
16.			x			x
17.			x			
18.			x	x	x	x
19.				x		
20.				x		
21.				x	x	
22.					x	
23.					x	
24.					x	
25.						x
26.						x

BIBLIOGRAPHIC ESSAY

The study of strategy can take the reader into virtually every field of scholarship, including the sciences, technology, economics, sociology, psychology, and history, to name but a few. Some of this material is synthesized in regular publications from organizations such as the International Institute of Strategic Studies, and in scholarly journals such as *Armed Forces & Society* and *Defense Analysis*. Readers interested in acquiring some basic knowledge of American military history can start by consulting Millett and Maslowski's *For the Common Defense*[27] or, for a simpler and less sophisticated examination, the U.S. Army's official text.[28] There are also several works on American military thought.[29]

---

27. Allan R. Millett and Peter Maslowski, *For the Common Defense: A Military History of the United States of America* (New York: Macmillan, 1984).

28. Center of Military History, *American Military History* (Washington, DC: Government Printing Office, 1988).

29. Among the classics on the subject was Walter Millis, ed., *American Military Thought* (Indianapolis: Bobbs-Merrill, 1966), although this work is out of date for anything much beyond the Korean war. A fine if dated work that combines strategic thought and military history is Russell F. Weigley's *The American Way of War: A History of United States Military Strategy and Policy* (Bloomington: Indiana University Press, 1977).

Surveys of Western and world military history abound.[30] Those interested in current global conflicts and threats but on a tight schedule may wish to consult a recent strategic atlas, such as those prepared by Keegan and Wheatcroft,[31] and by Chaliand and Rageau.[32] The end of the Cold War overtook many of these publications; only the most recent have much practical value.

Those with a beginning interest in strategy might do well to begin reading the classics. These include unabridged publications of famous writers, and edited collections with commentaries. Among the most useful collections is Chaliand's *The Art of War in World History,* [33] a massive compendium that includes excerpts from many often overlooked non-Western sources. Inevitably, the selections are brief and episodic. Other recommended colllections include Sawyer's anthology of Chinese strategists[34] and Liddell Hart's somewhat selective *The Sword and the Pen.*[35] Complete writings of individual famous leaders and strategists are easily found, usually with annotations and explanations by a current scholar. Numerous editions of Carl von Clausewitz's *On War* and Niccolo Machiavelli's *The Prince* are available. Clausewitz was both a strategist and a philosopher of war, and his tome has achieved a recent revival in U.S. military circles. His famous book (edited and published by his widow) is complex and dense, and hence is frequently misunderstood and quoted out of context. Machiavelli is more of interest to those

---

30. An erudite survey was J.F.C. Fuller, *A Military History of the Western World* (New York: Funk and Wagnalls, 1954–57). It exists in many different editions and abridgments. For pre-1800 military history generally, the best brief overview is Frederick Baumgartner's *From Spear to Flintlock: A History of War in Europe and the Middle East to the French Revolution* (New York: Praeger, 1991).

31. John Keegan and Andrew Wheatcroft, *Zones of Conflict: An Atlas of Future Wars* (London: Cape, 1986).

32. Gerard Chaliand and Jean-Pierre Rageau, *Strategic Atlas: A Comparative Geopolitics of the World's Powers,* 3rd edn. (New York: HarperCollins, 1992).

33. Gerard Chaliand, *The Art of War in World History: From Antiquity to the Nuclear Age* (Berkeley: University of California Press, 1994).

34. Ralph D. Sawyer, ed., *The Seven Military Classics of Ancient China* (Boulder, CO: Westview Press, 1993).

35. B. H. Liddell Hart and Adrian Liddell Hart, *The Sword and the Pen: Selections From the World's Greatest Military Writings* (New York: Thomas Crowell, 1976).

studying the overall strategy of statecraft, as opposed to military strategy. Other classics worth consulting—and these represent only the tip of the strategic iceberg—include the writings of Frederick the Great[36] and— a very recent "classic"—Mao Ze Dong.[37] Frederick is interesting because he bridges the transition from eighteenth-century to "modern" warfare and has a crucial impact on the wars of the French Revolution. Mao's ideas form a critical bridge between early Marxist thought on war (developed by Marx's co-author, Friedrich Engels) and revolutions in Third World peasant societies. In addition, Maoist thinking guided the North Vietnamese and Viet Cong leadership; no one can study the Vietnam War without considering Mao's thinking.

Then there are the works published in the last half-century intended to guide strategists in the Cold War and beyond. At risk of facing calumny and opprobrium from some of my professional colleagues, I highly recommend reading some of Liddell Hart's work, especially *Strategy*. True, Liddell Hart was tireless in the pursuit of materials that would prove his point, and establish his own importance, but his writings can stimulate broad-based, comprehensive thought about strategy to an extent that few others can. In addition, his skills as a writer were outstanding.[38] On this side of the pond, recent significant writers on strategy include Edward N. Luttwak,[39] the equally prolific Colin S. Gray (whose latest work on strategy will be published in 1998[40]), and Col. Harry G.

---

36. Jay Luvaas, ed., *Frederick the Great on the Art of War* (New York: The Free Press, 1966).

37. Samuel Griffith, tr., *Mao Tse-Tung on Guerrilla Warfare* (New York: Praeger, 1961).

38. B. H. Liddell Hart, *Strategy* (New York: Praeger, 1954). There are other editions as well. Liddell Hart's reputation has recently been rehabilitated. See Azar Gat, "British Influence and the Evolution of the Panzer Arm: Myth or Reality?" *War in History* 4 (Nos. 2 and 3, 1997): 150–173, 316–338.

39. See for example, Edward N. Luttwak, *The Pentagon and the Art of War: The Question of Military Reform* (New York: Simon and Schuster, 1984); Luttwak, *On the Meaning of Victory: Essays on Strategy* (New York: Simon and Schuster, 1986); Luttwak, *The Endangered American Dream* (New York: Simon and Schuster, 1994); Luttwak, *Strategy: The Logic of War and Peace* (Cambridge: Harvard University Press, March 1990)

40. Colin S. Gray, *Explorations in Strategy* (Westport, CT: Greenwood, 1998).

Summers,[41] who launched his career by applying Clausewitzian thought to the Vietnam War.[42] Summers' views are important because they reflect a considerable body of military opinion.[43] Soviet (and probably post-Soviet) strategy can be studied by reading one of the editions of the semi-official *Soviet Military Strategy* and—more important, perhaps—*Concept, Algorithm, Decision,* which describes the theory behind the decision-making.[44]

Finally, there are a number of modern studies of strategy and military thought worth considering. The best-known compendium study is *Makers of Modern Strategy,* revised and reissued over several decades to keep up with a changing world.[45] Its position in the strategic-academic marketplace has been challenged by *The Making of Strategy,*[46] which offers the reader a more thematic approach. The most recent comprehensive treatment of military thought through Clausewitz can be found in Azar Gat's work.[47] The fundamentals of great-power politics have been explained in a plethora of books, but few achieved the fame or readership of Paul Kennedy's *The Rise and Fall of the Great Powers.*[48] A broad approach to the problem of conflict can be found in Donald Kagan's 1995 book.[49] A seminal work in the modern study of crises is Graham T.

---

41. Harry G. Summers, *The New World Strategy: A Military Policy for America's Future* (New York: Simon and Schuster, 1995).

42. Harry G. Summers, *On Strategy: A Critical Analysis of the Vietnam War* (Novato, CA: Presidio, 1982).

43. See for example, Bruce Palmer Jr., *The 25-Year War: America's Military Role in Vietnam* (New York: Simon and Schuster, 1984).

44. Valentin Vasil Druzhinin and D. S. Kontorov, *Concept, Algorithm, Decision* (Washington, DC: Government Printing Office, 1975).

45. Peter Paret, ed., *Makers of Modern Strategy: From Machiavelli to the Nuclear Age* (Princeton, NJ: Princeton University Press, 1986). The first edition was edited by Edward Meade Earle in 1943.

46. Williamson Murray, MacGregor Knox, and Alvin Bernstein, eds., *The Making of Strategy: Rulers, States, and War* (New York: Cambridge University Press, 1995).

47. Azar Gat, *The Origins of Military Thought: From the Enlightenment to Clausewitz* (New York: Oxford University Press, 1991).

48. Paul Kennedy, *The Rise and Fall of the Great Powers: Economic Change and Military Conflict from 1500 to 2000* (New York: Random House, 1989).

49. Donald Kagan, *On the Origins of War and the Preservation of Peace* (New York: Doubleday, 1995).

Allison's *Essence of Decision,*[50] although its conclusions have been dated by recent revelations concerning the Cuban Missile Crisis. Modern efforts to quantify and rationalize the subject of military conflict are represented by T. N. Dupuy's *Numbers, Predictions and War.*[51] Unfortunately for Dupuy and many other writers on strategy who have sought to impose order on the chaos of war, their approach has been seriously undermined by the publication of Roger Beaumont's *War, Chaos and History.*[52] Beaumont's focus on the disorder of conflict is especially relevant to one of the points made in this book—the difficulty of engaging in detailed planning.

---

50. Graham T. Allison, *Essence of Decision: Explaining the Cuban Missile Crisis* (Boston: Little, Brown, 1971).

51. T. N. Dupuy, *Numbers, Predictions and War: Using History to Evaluate Combat Factors and Predict the Outcome of Battle* (Indianapolis: Bobbs-Merrill, 1979).

52. Roger A. Beaumont, *War, Chaos and History* (Westport, CT: Praeger, 1994).

INDEX

About the Author

HUBERT P. VAN TUYLL is Associate Professor of History at Augusta State University. His previous publications include *Feeding the Bear: American Aid to the Soviet Union, 1941–1945* (Greenwood, 1989) as well as a number of articles on various military-historical topics.

ISBN 0-313-30674-5
90000>
EAN
9 780313 306747
HARDCOVER BAR CODE